EX LIBRIS

June E Peterson

Madame of the Heights

the story of a prostitute's progress

by Marianne Hancock

A WINDSWEPT BOOK

Printed in the United States of America
for the Publisher.

WINDSWEPT HOUSE PUBLISHERS
P.O. Box 159
Mt. Desert, Maine 04660

Madame sat for her portrait and had lithographs made for reproduction. Her decolletage was modest, but age enforced no other sanction. In the Biblioteque Nationale that lithograph is listed as Madame Burr, Widow of the late Aaron Burr, Vice President of the United States, formerly Madame Jumel, heroine of New York.

Portrait of Madam Jumel with grand-niece and grand-nephew. Painted in Rome by Alcide Ercole, 1854. Used with permission of The Morris-Jumel Mansion and Museum.

To my daughters, Mandy and Ann.

Madame of the Heights

the story of a prostitute's progress

Forward

This is the history of Betsy Bowen who was born in a brothel in 1775, who became a celebrated courtesan and who was, briefly, the wife of Aaron Burr. There are gaps in Madame's early life, and where the evidence totters between fact and legend I have favored fact.

The record of the contest for Madame's fortune, as it was determined by the Supreme Court of the United States, is in the National Archives in Washington. D.C. There is a full account of the litigation in New York courts in the New York Public Library. The tragedy of Madame's mother is borne out by the historical records of Providence. The New York Historical Society has, in conjunction with the Burr Papers, many of the letters between Madame Jumel and her first husband Stephen. I have admiration tempered with awe for the intuition of Pauline Stone who translated Stephen's heretofore undeciphered letters.

I have sometimes condensed and reorganized journal entries, depositions, testimony and letters, but I have put no unrecorded words in anyone's mouth. I wrote of Madame as if I were playing a part; and as an actress playing Lady Macbeth must justify what that lady does, so I have tried to understand Madame Jumel as she understood herself.

I am grateful for **The Jumel Mansion**, written by the Mansion's first curator, William Henry Shelton, to whom I owe the stories Madame told her adolescent court, as well as Mlle. Nitschke's account of Madame's ghost; and I am grateful to Jane Crowley, the curator

1

who let me work at a desk in the hall of the Mansion. Like Madame Nitschke, I was sometimes aware of Madame's ghost.

The story of Nathan Hale's arson is fully documented. (I have kept those records separately.) The letters of Mary Hassals are in the New York Public Library. James Parton's **The Life and Times of Aaron Burr** is a seminal biography. Burr's own journals, **The Memoirs of Aaron Burr**, edited by his executor, Mathew L. Davis was of similar value.

1

"Perhaps what starts out as a dream turns into a drive ,
- takes on a reality of its own. Is that not a cousin to
destiny?'
Margaret George

Madame, who was born in the first year of the
American Revolution, died in the last year of the Civil
War. On July seventeenth, this obituary appeared in
the New York Times: *"Madame Eliza Brown Jumel
died on Saturday in the ninetieth year of her age at her late
residence in Washington Heights. During the morning
her remains were exposed in a rosewood coffin to view in
the parlor, in which were gathered a circle of friends...
Shortly after one o'clock, the coffin was removed to the
Church of the Intercession where the burial service was
performed by the Rev. H. S. Smith. She died possessed of a
considerable fortune which her grandchildren will
doubtless inherit."*
    She did indeed die possessed of a fortune. Her
relations would fight for it for many years. She had
two grandchildren, although in all likelihood she did
not know it, and they would inherit nothing. In her
last will and testament she disowned with token
bequests everyone she had ever known.
    The litigation that ensued as Madame's would-
be heirs fought for her fortune lasted for sixteen years.
Because of the explosive question of illegitimacy
(whether a bastard could inherit from his mother) it
was decided at last and negatively by the Supreme
Court of the United States. The case, known as the
Jumel Will Case, was sensational as well as long. For as

Madame's bastard, who thought of himself as the natural son of George Washington, proved his own identity, he revealed his mother's.

It was commonly known at the time of her death that Madame was the widow of Stephen Jumel, a Frenchman, a merchant prince of the city of New York; and that her second husband had been Aaron Burr, the third Vice President of the United States.

A great many people knew the legends that had accrued to her name. It was said that she was the great courtesan of the new republic, a favorite of the Bonapartes, that she caused the duel between Hamilton and Burr, that she murdered Stephen Jumel, that she was the richest woman in the United States, and that she was the only woman in the world to sleep with both Washington and Napoleon.

In truth, she lived on the fringe of history and the threads of legend and reality are tangled. She was indeed responsible for the political disgrace of Hamilton and, had her intrigues succeeded, she would have sailed with Napoleon to America in 1815. Probably she killed Stephen Jumel; and in her fashion, she was familiar with kings and emperors.

But Madame kept no diary, and the men she did or did not sleep with had no inclination to record their night with her. For it was also known that she was born in a brothel, child of a whore and a sailor; and that until she learned to exploit men, she followed her mother's trade.

The Court which sat in judgment on her would-be heirs, and incidentally on herself, were not unkind to Madame. Obviously they believed, as she had, that wealth and worth were synonymous. *"Yes, early in life she was wrecked,"* the Honorable Chauncey Shaffer told

4

the Supreme Court. *"Brought up among loose, immoral people with evil examples around her and foul associations of the lowest grade - Indians, Negroes and Whites all herded together... But she was not one of the wrecked ones who float downstream to become loathsome weeds on the strand.*

By a miracle of miracles, a reversal of human nature, she was saved and lifted to a life of splendor, more like the elevation of a prisoner to the Chair of State in an Eastern country than anything in the natural growth of our Republic."

Madame saved and lifted herself. She was an archetypal courtesan, pleasing and, if she could, manipulating the men she knew. As Betsy Bowen, Eliza Capet, Madame de la Croix and Eliza Brown - for she changed names with her circumstances - she captivated men. As Madame Jumel and Madame Burr, she ruled them.

The age offered no other satisfaction. No woman could command respect without the protection of a man's name or in the reflected glory of his position. Madame never thought it could be otherwise. As she grew old and ego took precedence over sexuality, she was, in her own right, a person of power, a femme sole as her legal papers would attest.

She was always flamboyant, indomitably amoral. She was also lonely, frustrated and ridiculous. Her maternal longings were never appeased. She endlessly yearned for little George Washington, the son she gave away. The surrogate families she hired to replace her own were less kind than her true kin. In the vanities of her old age she was sadder than Lear, without a fool to tell her the truth and without Cordelia to love her.

At the time of her death, the true story of Madame's life was remembered by a handful of old men

5

and women in Providence, who had known her as Betsy Bowen; who had known her mother Phebe, and her sister Polly; who knew her son George Washington Bowen on whose behalf they testified.

The tragedy of Madame's mother was a cautionary force. Phebe could not protect her children from the stigma of the Old Gaol, which was a whore house, or the Workhouse where they were taken when Phebe was in prison or driven from town to town. They shared their mother's humiliation and jeopardy. Betsy triumphed over circumstances that destroyed her mother. But her grandiosity as Madame Jumel was a mask for self-doubt and her amorality, a stunting of natural development.

It is expedient then to turn to the testimony of the old people who knew Madame as Betsy Bowen, and to the ancient archives of Providence that record the ordeals of the Bowen women.

2

"One for the rook, one for the crow, one to die, and
one to grow."
Farmers Almanac

George Washington Bowen had no better
witness than his friend Daniel Hull, who believed
Phebe was his aunt; and Polly and Betsy, who played
with him as a child, were his cousins.

Old Hull was ingenuous; and although lawyers
for the opposition harassed him, trying to make him
seem self serving or at least senile, his openness was
disarming. *"I admit it,"* he said. *"My memory has failed
me for about a dozen years, but I can remember what
happened when I was a boy better than what happened two
years ago. All the trouble with me, if you want to know, is
that I have the bleeding piles. Once in a while I'm taken
bleeding and it nearly kills me. Sometimes it nearly kills
me. Sometimes it nearly kills me here in court."*

The court led him back to the time Betsy and
Polly Bowen were his playmates and he thought of
their mother as his aunt. He was asked to describe
Aunt Phebe, Betsy's mother, but he was not used to
framing such things in words and could not easily
articulate his memory.

*"Phebe Bowen was a good-sized woman, rather
slimmish, medium height ,"* he said. *"It appears to me she
was light complexioned. Her hair was not black but kind
of tannish. A common nose, I couldn't say what shape.
She was just one of them loose characters."*

The records of Providence bear Hull out.
Phebe Bowen was a prostitute. Probably her mother

was too, for she left Phebe to be sold at pauper auction when she was five years old.

Three groups of people were bought and sold in the eighteenth century: black slaves, bound servants and paupers, who because of age or illness could not care for their own needs. For all their piety, the settling fathers rewarded avarice. Paupers were not, like other human merchandise, sold to the highest bidder; but to the lowest, to the family who agreed to maintain them at the least possible cost to the town, often to the family who would provide the least food and greatest neglect.

Mistress James Lovette kept Phebe for eight years, until she was pregnant with her first child, begotten by John Bowen, a sailor from nearby Cumberland in Rhode Island. When Phebe found herself pregnant, she changed her name to Bowen, for only a married woman could hope to survive in Colonial society. But John Bowen could not or would not help her. She had her baby alone, called him John Thomas Bowen and unable to do otherwise, wandered on. She was thirteen years old. When she was fifteen and examined by the Council of Providence, she had been passed from hand to hand by seven men. This confession, taken in dictation by the town fathers of Providence on January 27, 1769, is the first formal notice taken of the mother of the woman who would become Madame Jumel: *"I don't know where I was born. I come from Tauton. I removed nine years agon to this town and lived with my sister that married Timothy Rind. But before I come to this place I lived with John Owens that is now North Providence and after my sister removed from Providence, I lived with John Brown the rigger. And then I went with Abraham Whipple. From*

thence I went to dwell with James Scott. And from Scott I went and lived with John Nash, and from there back to Scott. And now I live with David Wilkinson.
Phebe
Her X Mark
Bowen. "

The town fathers, who met and dined in Whipple's Tavern added their judgment to the document. *"Whereas the said Phebe Bowen be and is hereby rejected from being an inhabitant of this town. "*

Without John Bowen's support, Phebe had no alternative. She was forced to live as a prostitute. If a man or some established brothel took her in, since it cost them nothing, the town fathers might look away. But her jeopardy was endless. She could be driven from any town - from town to town.

The righteous men of Providence had a paranoid fear of any stranger who might become a public charge. The laws against vagrants were harsh, lengthy and often revised for greater precision. Rogues, vagabonds, prostitutes, the lewd, idle, or dissolute; those who might beg, steal, lie or curse; who might corrupt manners, debauch youth or encourage slaves to pilfer; jugglers, gamblers, palmists and any persons claiming occult power were warned out.

A stranger coming to Providence had to announce his presence and intentions within forty days. If he lacked a certificate from his last place of residence, he had to remove unless a resident posted bond; and the town fathers were suspicious of bondsmen, afraid that the cunning insinuations of strangers might overcome the bondsmen's good judgment. They reserved the right to remove any

9

person they did not like or any person tainted with bad fame.

Anyone harboring or hiding a stranger for thirty days was fined four shillings, the cost of holding the stranger until he could be removed. If a stranger was not warned out, he had to come before the Council at the end of a year's grace with proof that he had either purchased land worth forty pound or completed an apprenticeship. An apprentice's term was arduous. He served his master as a bound servant; forbidden to marry, absent himself from the village, go to a tavern, to drink or play cards until he was released. The Council of Providence did not act with undue harshness when they warned Phebe out. Whores were often whipped.

Phebe found shelter in the brothel run by Margaret Fairchild, the freed slave of Major Fairchild. It was a New England custom to free a slave begotten by her master on her twenty-fourth birthday. The records say nothing about the relationship of Major Fairchild and his Margaret, but apparently he backed her enterprise because she had money enough to rent the Old Gaol and to take both white and black whores under her protection.

The Old Gaol had been empty for years. The Gaoler and his wife had resented carrying water and food up the steep hill to their charges. The New Gaol was down by the docks, built into the mud on piles overhanging tidal water.

Providence rises sharply from the waterfront. The high streets are lined with dignified and commodious houses, but the lower streets were squalid. Swamps had been filled, the natural drainage blocked, and the lowlands were covered with stagnant water

10

which bred malaria and yellow fever in summer, and in all seasons were redolent of that filth which breeds typhoid. Shipping excepted, the business of Providence was distilling rum for the slave trade. Like the New Gaol, the stills hung over the water, and at half-tide herds of half-wild hogs rooted in the refuse grain and wallowed in the slime.

Streetwalkers, who found their customers in the lower town, were in for the night by ten. Nights were dark. Candles and lamps were for the gentry. Poor people burned pitch-pine knots or made dips with odds and ends of cooking fat. In 1775 a night watch was organized and four men patrolled the streets in pairs from ten until sunrise, ringing their bells and calling *ALL'S WELL,* if indeed, it was. By ten the Old Gaol was loud with revelry.

Before the Revolution only outcasts frequented the brothel; Indians, half-breeds and sailors. It was a Colonial axiom that sailors were sinful; that they had tested all the vices of the world in their travels and carried corruption like a contagious disease.

Phebe bore two children in the Old Gaol; Polly who was born in 1773 and Betsy, who would become Madame Jumel, in 1775. In spite of the circumstances of their birth, both children were baptized in the proudest building in Providence, the great stone Baptist church - evidence that Phebe hoped to raise them in grace.

In that year of tension, 1775, Providence was uneasy, but passionately anti-British. Tories were added to the list of persons to be warned out. Two merchants considered themselves warned when their shutters and doors were sealed with tar and feathers. The Council invited all lovers of freedom to a tea

11

party: *"To cast into the fire a needless herb which for a long time hath been highly detrimental to our Liberty, Interest and Health."* While bells rang, young men blacked the India Company's sign with tar, and set fire to three hundred pounds of tea on Congress Commons. Everyone who watched was exhilarated by their daring, the flames and the night. Prostitutes in the Old Gaol profited.

As a city at the head of navigable water, Providence imagined itself in great danger. As war began, Newport across the harbor was occupied; while refugees from Newport fled to Providence, Providence families fled to the interior. The town became an armed camp. There were warships in the harbor and a company of artillery in the college. Business ground to a halt, and except for the din of arms and martial music in the distance, the lower streets were silent and deserted.

Food was scarce that winter and with the scarcity, the price of common necessities was inflated. Corn sold for twenty dollars a bushel and rye for twenty-five. The Council imported a hundred bushels of corn and twelve of rye which they doled out to the poor. Still the brothel prospered.

The whores were kind to Phebe's daughters and spelled themselves as communal mothers. In these annals the poor are good to each other. Soldiers and sailors are famously fond of children. They made pets of the Bowen girls.

A hungry, neglected baby learns things a cosseted child need never know; how to direct her energies toward survival, to be aggressive for food and love, or a place by the fire. A child used to hunger understands <u>no more</u> and does not complain. Betsy may have been a dirty, snot-nosed baby, but her marvelous eyes, her vivacity and intelligence delighted her mother's customers.

She learned a baby's wiles early; the hugged shoulders, the shiver of mock ecstasy that would make a man pop something in her mouth. By trial and error she learned how much defiance, sauciness, mimicry - what words or snatches of songs would make an adult amiable. Madame would speak fondly of her habit of stamping her foot and tossing her head. She learned the charm of that mannerism in The Old Gaol.

Betsy demanded her mother's love and attention. Perhaps for a while she tried to push men away from Phebe, saying, "No, my Mama," for she needed and claimed things called mine. She might offer a man her treasures; a blanket, a rag, a kitten, a doll, even a bite from her mouth, saying "Mine," teasing a man as she had been teased.

At one, Betsy knew enough to hide in a corner and keep quiet when she was afraid, to curl with cats to keep warm, to rock in bed while a man and woman made love. Because frozen clothes are painful, she learned in one winter not to wet herself. Without other children to play with, Polly and Betsy learned to play with wandering animals, hungry dogs and cats, even half-wild hogs, without being afraid.

A child's fears may be projected by rote. At two and three Betsy was afraid of the dark, of the sound of muskets and cannon, of thunder and rain, and separation from Phebe. At four she was afraid of the dark, the noise of guns and of Phebe dying. Suddenly at five, she was sure of herself and, having by nature the qualities of a survivor, she loved the Old Gaol and thought it the best of all possible worlds.

13

That year of the Cold Winter, in 1780, the tide of war changed. The threat of British invasion receded and the whores in Providence were forgiven their sins. In July the Comte de Rochambeau anchored his ships and disembarked with six thousand men, thus tripling the population of Providence; and these Frenchmen addressed themselves to the women of the town with the foreign soldiers' time-honored greeting: "*Voulez-vous accouchez avec moi?*" No men in Providence begrudged the prosperity of the prostitutes whose presence protected the virtue of their wives and daughters.

The foreign soldiers dug underground huts for themselves in North Providence. This was no rag-tag, bob-tail army of farmers. Rochambeau commanded the military elite of France and his officers were welcomed in private homes of the upper town. Five-year-old Betsy began to speak French.

This was the happiest season of her childhood. Her home was secure. Her mother and the women around her were in high spirits; and the Frenchmen with their mystery and glamour, saw that the occupants of the Old Gaol had food and fuel, perhaps even luxuries - candles and mirrors.

In May 1781, Washington came to Providence to confer with Rochambeau, who with exquisite tact, placed himself and his men at Washington's disposal. It was time out of war, a week of spontaneous gaiety, torch-light parades, balls and parties. If the same linen, silver, candelabra and mirrors appeared on every occasion, the effect was no less splendid.

Washington led every dance with pretty Peggy Champlain; Innocent's Reel, the Arcadian Nuptials, Boston's Delight, Love and Opportunity, the Innocent

Maid, the Soldier's Pay... round dances all. But he took time to visit the home of Reuben Ballou, a dispatch rider who "lay very low" after a fall from his horse.

Never a social man, never at ease with strangers, lacking in small talk and shy with women, the General took tea and dinner with the Ballous on several occasions. The Ballou house was his refuge in Providence and it was here that six-year-old Betsy met the great man for whom she would name her son. Freelove Ballou was her Aunt Free, and Betsy was sent to the Ballou household to wait on the General.

It is hard to be sure of the relationship between Freelove and Betsy. Aunt was commonly used to mean Missus, a married woman lower in the social order than Mistress, but higher than Goody or Mother. Yet Freelove and Reuben were so consistently loyal to Phebe and her children that one must assume a blood relationship.

Betsy was old enough to find the situation wonderful. She stamped her foot and tossed her head like a little colt. The General let himself be captivated by the child of the house. Madame Jumel's remarkable image of herself as a seducer of heroes began then, with the conquest of the exhausted General, for like all children, she found her self-worth in the appraisal of others.

In July, before he joined Washington and marched with him to Yorktown, Rochambeau gave a ball to thank Providence for its hospitality and to bid farewell to its ladies and gentlemen. At sunrise, for the dance lasted all night, many a young woman and her gallant found parting painful. Thus, like any army, the French departed, leaving the women who had assuaged

15

their loneliness, sadder - and in this case wiser. For the French brought condoms with them made, like sausage casings, from the intestines of animals. Thereafter, according to Moureau St. Mery, who in his journal recorded things Americans could not even speak of, women demanded that apothecaries publicly display these contraceptives.

But the fastidious Frenchmen found many things distasteful. *"American women do not tell their daughters about menstruation for below the waist they admit only ankles... They do not wash the linen so used, and think Frenchwomen reprehensible for having different customs. They have but one colored skirt which serves always in this capacity until it must be thrown away... Nor do they keep their chemises clean, but dirty them with those marks of that need to which nature subjects every animal."*

In the Old Gaol hauling and heating water was always arduous; and as the whores struggled to meet the Frenchmen's standards of cleanliness, contraception and menstruation were surely discussed with Polly and Betsy.

3

"Poverty is a great enemy of human happiness; it certainly destroys liberty, and it makes some virtues impractical and others extremely difficult."
Samuel Johnson. 1782

When the French departed prostitutes were no longer tolerated. Providence was bitter about the ravages of war. *"Our port has been blockaded for more than twelve months. Our stores and shops are almost empty, our navigation demolished, our shipping at an end, our houses already standing empty and going to decay by slow degrees - or more suddenly and wantonly ruined by troops barracking in them. And many foreign residents among us, and our most wealthy inhabitants who made the principal figures in our trade have packed their fortunes and removed to places of greater security. The common sort of people who are left behind are mostly out of employment and the poor among us have to be supported by the remaining persons of property. We do not mention the shipping which lies rotting in our harbor..."* So wrote the Council of Providence.

Betsy was seven when the French army left. Again she was afraid of many things: of the dark garret and root cellar, of dead men's ghosts and witches, of enemy soldiers and spies, of Phebe dying, of splinters and nosebleeds... It never occurred to her to fear the people of Providence, but their enmity made her nightmares trivial. *"When the Old Gaol House of Ill Fame was torn down By the Mob and Burned,"* say the annals, *"there were in the House and removed Phebe Bowen and her daughter Betsy and an other named Polly*

17

and a Negro named Black Betts and a Mulatto of about eighteen named Esther. "

The mob had not celebrated in such a fashion since the tea party of 1775. Burning tea had tested the young men's courage but burning the brothel was equally exhilarating. It was safe enough, and their prowess was proved by wailing children and terrified women.

Phebe found work again in the quieter whorehouse of Patience Ingrahm. But Polly and Betsy were taken from her and put in the Workhouse under the direction of Nathaniel Wheaton, Overseer to the Poor. As prisons were later designed to discourage crime and reform criminals, so the Workhouse was designed to discourage poverty and reform paupers. *"Poverty and Ruin are most often owed to an Idle and Vicious course,"* begins the Articles of the Workhouse. In spite of that, it was the last resort of the blind, limbless, maimed, old men, orphaned children, bastards and women expecting them. It was the last refuge of anyone too wretched to be sold at pauper auction.

The common work of the House was to pick oakum; to twist and pull old ropes apart for ship's caulking. The punishments visited on those who for one reason or another failed to pick their quota of oakum, were cruel and common. Those who were slothful, who loitered or were idle or absent from their place of work, who feigned illness, who lied to the Overseer, swore, quarreled, wasted materials, tried to escape, misused tools, profaned the Sabbath, or missed Divine Service, who behaved lasciviously, or acted irregularly or immorally were gagged, forced to wear a wooden yoke around their necks or on both feet, or put in irons, or kept in the dungeon on bread and water, according to the judgment of the Overseer.

Like Indians whose souls were worth saving but whose lives were not, the souls of the poor were provided for. Every morning and evening the Overseer read Divine Scripture and discoursed on Divinity, and before every meal the inmates thanked God for his mercy.

There were specific provisions for children. Polly and Betsy were given new clothes and a woman was assigned to look after them, to see that nits were picked from their heads, and that they washed their faces and combed their hair in the morning.

Then, although the idea of infecting one's blood with a loathsome disease was more than most Americans could endure, the Bowen children were inoculated against smallpox. Holding Betsy and Polly in turn, Wheaton opened veins in the crooks of their arms, prepared the wounds with mercury, and dressed them with matter from pustules of pox, which like an artist's gold dust, he kept in a double scallop shell. *"We talk of freedom,"* wrote a Providence woman, *"and most of us are free enough. But the poor are inoculated whether they will or no."*

Polly and Betsy were left in the barn, for inoculation fever was as contagious as smallpox. They vomited in the morning and felt better by evening. Pustules the size of peas erupted on their bodies. *"To excite revulsion in their superior parts,"* the Overseer drew blood from their feet, and as their fever diminished, he gave them doses of glauber salts *"to promote a gentle but constant discharge from their bowels."* Trembling and white they picked their quota of oakum.

In the fall the children were back with Phebe,

19

who still lived with Patience Ingrahm. But complaints were lodged against Ingrahm's brothel, and the two women were committed to Gaol until someone gave bond for their future conduct. For the first time the Council of Providence appointed Henry Bowen, the Town Sergeant, to take charge of Phebe's worldly goods, *"to take them in his care except it be advisable to furnish her with bedding suitable for her circumstances."* Thus she was left with a corn-husk mattress and appropriate blankets.

The Bowen children were in and out of the Workhouse four times, until they were finally bound out to work for their keep. But from this time on, for three different periods of three months each, Polly and Betsy were tutored in reading at the expense of Henry Bowen. The receipts are in the annals of Providence: *"Received of Henry Bowen, Town Sergeant, eighteen shillings in return for the schooling of his two daughters, Polly and Betsy, Henry Bowen, Town Sergeant."*

Perhaps Bowen, the Sergeant, owed Phebe a debt of guilt. Perhaps he was touched by the spirit and intelligence of the Bowen girls. Whatever the reason, the man who would so often escort Phebe to Gaol, paid for the education of her daughters.

John Bowen, the sailor, Phebe's so-called husband died in 1786. His obituary appeared in the Providence Gazette and Country Journal: *"John Bowen, a sea-faring man of this town was knocked overboard by the boom of a fishing vessel and drowned in the Harbor of Newport on Monday last, the 17thh of May."* Providence was full of Bowens, but the terseness of the obituary clearly separates the drowned man from the eminent families in the upper town.

The Council paid seven shillings to dig John

Bowen's grave; three shillings for the use of a black cart, decorated with skulls and thigh bones, to haul him to the cemetery; an additional three shillings to the grave digger. The corpse was committed to the earth without psalm or prayer. Phebe and her daughters were not present.

Bond for Phebe's good behavior was paid by Washington's dispatch rider, Reuben Ballou who took her into his household. Two years later, on the day after Christmas, Phebe bore another daughter. In all likelihood she did not know the father of her baby. The child was delivered by Freelove Ballou.

Freelove was not a righteous woman. She was a doctoress, and to add to Reuben's income, she rented rooms to whores and their men. Reuben and Freelove were not respectable, but they were responsible. Rich families gave slave babies away like kittens, but among the poor, kin cared for kin.

Phebe's fourth child was named Lavinia Ballou, and the Ballous raised her as their own child. Thus of Phebe's four children, John Thomas and Lavinia were given away. Polly would die in childbirth, or from some other hazard of her trade. Betsy flourished, as if she were not diminished by the circumstances of her birth. But she carried such wounds to her pride that the value she placed on herself was corrupted.

The families who took Betsy and Polly in as bound girls did not keep them long. Visitors from Europe were appalled by the license given American children, at their arrogance and rudeness. No one gentled the Bowen girls. Colonel Sam Adams, to whom Betsy was bound, was obliged by law to provide her with good food and lodging. His pretty wife instructed her slaves to teach the waif the

21

womanly arts. Betsy learned more from Mistress Adams than from her slaves. This was the first time Betsy had seen a woman surrounded by wealth and protected by a man. The gulf between the life men led her mother and the comfort of the Colonel's wife was stunning.

In the Workhouse of Old Gaol or at Mother Ballou's, tables were set with pewter and wood. Two or three ate from a common dish and everyone drank beer from the quart pot. Mistress Adams set her table with Liverpool ware, silver and linen. Her punch was made from Madeira, and when a ship came in from the Indies, she added the juice of fresh limes. Working women seldom took their aprons off. Mistress Adams wore a silk dress with ruffles which covered her wrists. And her hair, which was rolled back over a rat, gleamed like the crupper of a saddle. Phebe's customers wore leather-wash britches above bare legs. The gentlemen at the White Horse Tavern, which belonged to Colonel Adams, wore stocking and their shoes had silver buckles.

The gentlemen who frequented the White Horse to exchange news of the sea and keep pace with the times, were slavers. The buying and selling of slaves had been outlawed in Rhode Island, but slave ships continued their profitable rounds; picking up rum in Providence to be exchanged for molasses in the West Indies, to be exchanged for slaves on the Guinea coast of Africa, to be sold in the American south. Although these merchants were Sons of Liberty, and although what they did was immoral in principle and nauseating in practice, they were not conscious of wrong doing. The captain who praised God in his account book, *"Thank God for another cargo of benighted beings come to a land where they can learn the benefits of the Gospel,"* spoke for the men at the White Horse. Few doubted that slaves had souls or that the saving of souls justified the subjugation of their bodies.

Betsy absorbed the philosophy of these men without question, and the visible rewards of slavers impressed her.

American women bloomed early. At twelve Betsy was full bosomed. Her extraordinary eyes were blue with some pigmentation; men called them violet.

Her hair, which would become as dark as mahogany, was bright as the coat of a fox. Like her mother she was sexually initiated at puberty, and she learned as much from Colonel Adams or from his friends as she did from her Mistress. The wish to please is part of the will to survive and in the Adams household Betsy sensed the power her beauty could command and took pleasure in it.

But when Mistress Adams died, Betsy could not live as the Colonel's concubine. According to law, he dismissed her *"with decent clothing for all parts of her body."* Sometime in her twelfth year she moved back to the household of Freelove Ballou.

4

"A licentious commerce between the sexes may be
carried on by men without contaminating the mind so
as to render them unworthy of the marriage bed and
incapable of discharging the honorable duties of
husband, father, friend... But the contamination of the
female mind is the necessary and inseparable
consequence of illicit intercourse with men... Women
are universally virtuous or wholly undone."
Ladies Magazine. London, 1777

The Council, as they did whenever they
received complaints, examined Phebe again, and again
they warned her out. She told the fathers that she was
thirty, that Polly was fourteen and Betsy twelve. St.
Mery wrote that American women age rapidly. *They
fade at twenty-three. Their hair is thin, their teeth bad at
thirty. They are old at thirty-five, senile and decrepit by
forty.*" Phebe signed her deposition with a trembling
'X'. This time she moved with her daughters, to the
Old Warren Road on the outskirts of Providence, to an
abandoned hut where she tried to make a home.

This was the time Daniel Hull remembered
best. *"It was just an old hut,"* he told the court. *"I guess
it has all dropped and gone to pieces by now. But I used to
go there every Sunday with my father and mother because
we passed on our way to my grandfather's house. And
they was poor and we was poor. We used to bring them
cookies and my father used to bring them bread. We used
to stop right at the door and the girls used to come out.
They was young, you know and I was a small boy. They
used to think a deal of me. I was sort of their favorite and*

24

they was always after me. I don't know how old they was.
A boy can't tell ages. But I used to think she was my real
Aunt Phebe and used to call her so. No," he said in
answer to a question, *" I never saw Phebe abusing those*
girls. She might have done it, but if so I don't know it.

They all used to come in town and they used to
stop at our house. And Phebe would have a cart and bring
in yarbs and greens. They used to come in two or three
times a week. We used to give 'em bread and they'd go
begging."

But Polly and Betsy were streetwalkers, not
beggars. They brought their men to Mother Ballou's
who, according to custom, kept one dollar, half of their
wages. *"Missus Ballou used to keep a whore house then*
and the girls used to stay there sometimes, I know," said
old Hull.

The Bowen girls were welcome too in the inns
the Frenchmen had frequented, the Pidge Tavern near
the old campground and the Muddy Dock near Mother
Ballou's where cock fights were held even on the
Sabbath. The Golden Ball with its gilded globe had a
finer reputation. President Washington stayed there on
his sole visit to Providence, and the Frenchmen who
owned it had been officers in Rochaumbeau's army.
The Bowen sisters were not necessarily welcome there.
But remembering how French soldiers had made life
pleasant in the Old Gaol, Betsy was drawn to those
foreigners who remained in Providence.

"Well, we carried bread and things out there on
the Old Warren Road," Hull continued, *"until*
Narragansett Indians tore the hut to pieces and threw the
furniture out of it. We used to call it Narragansett
whenever the mob did anything bad. And after the mob
tore down that place, I guess they all went to live with

25

Peter d'Espre about a block from where I live. I believe he was a rigger. I know he had a boat and fixed her."

D'Espre was a Frenchman who stayed on in Providence after the war. He was a barber as well as a rigger, and he bred monkeys and so eked out his living with a tiny zoo. He tried to teach the monkeys tricks and scolded them in a conglomerate of French and English curses which small boys loved to mock.

He advertised in the <u>Gazette and Country Journal</u>: *"Natural curiosity. Monkey about three weeks old to be seen at the house of Peter de'Espre. This singular little animal merits the Attention of every curious Person and is perhaps the First of its kind ever seen in North America. His Face and Ears are white and very much resemble the Human Species. The Dam takes it in her Arms and walking on her Hind Feet about that room, presents it to the View of Every Spectator. Admittance Every Day of the Week, Sundays Excepted from Nine o'clock in the morning until Four o'clock in the Afternoon."* He charged nine pence.

Old Hull remembered the monkeys. *"They used to keep two or three monkeys there at d'Espre's house and I liked to see 'em. And when Betsy called me into the house, I went in.*

There was two women with Peter d'Espre, the Phebe I used to call my aunt and another. The other used to go off begging. You couldn't tell nothing about her. I couldn't tell you if d'Espre used to have more in his family. Women used to go there forward and backwards. I suppose he was married once. The talk was that his wife was dead."

Probably during the war when he was stationed in Providence, d'Espre came to know Phebe and her girls, for in addition to his business as a rigger, barber and monkey trainer, he acted as a procurer of prostitutes.

"And when Peter d'Espre left there that was the last time I ever seen him," said Hull. *"And the last time I saw Phebe was in the attic. And the last I saw Betsy there it was the time I didn't go across the little brook-like to see her monkey."* A monkey was a marvelous accessory for a whore. With such a creature on her shoulder any man could strike up a conversation.

One of the men Phebe met at d'Espre's was Jonathan Clarke from Boston. Like many veterans after the war, who found they were no longer compatible with their wives, or that their wives were committed to other relationships, Clarke was rootless. But when he fell in love with Phebe, he had left behind him in Massachusetts a wife and six children. In spite of that, in March 1790, Phebe and Jonathan called themselves married.

In Providence Clarke was never more than a laborer. Occasionally he worked for the town repairing roads. More often he was unemployed. Yet Phebe had reason to be proud of her new husband. He was an officer and a gentleman and carried his commission to prove it.

"To Jonathan Clarke, Gentleman: We, reposing special Trust and Confidence in your Patriotism, Valor, Conduct and Fidelity, do by these presents constitute and appoint you a second lieutenant in the Regiment of Artillery commanded by Colonel John Crane in the Army of the United States, raised for the Defense of Liberty and for the Repelling of Every Hostile Invasion thereof, this first day of February, Anno Domini, 1777, by Order of Congress. John Hancock, President."

Those splendid words, Gentleman, Trust,

Valor, Patriotism, and Fidelity comforted Phebe. They were solace to Betsy. Years later, traveling in the south as Madame Jumel, she found Clarke's commission. Together with two other fragments of her true past, Madame kept it hidden in the attic of her Mansion where it was found after her death.

Clarke was not a good provider and when he was first examined by the Council, he was warned out. Then, being feisty by nature, he challenged the town fathers, demanding satisfaction from Samuel Robinson who had assaulted him with *"fists and feet."* But the patience of the Council was at an end. They examined Clarke and his wife Phebe for the last time, and with the full force of the law, warned them out.

"It is therefore resolved that the said Jonathan Clarke and his said wife Phebe, be and they are, hereby rejected from being inhabitants of this town...

Resolved: Whereas Jonathan Clarke and his wife Phebe who have heretofore been removed by Order of the Council, have come into this town without leave or consent, they have incurred the penalty of fine and corporal punishment.

And whereas this Council on principles of humanity are willing that in case they immediately quit this town to remit the punishment they justly deserve; and it is hereby resolved that they are dismissed from the place of confinement, and in case they are at any time exceeding three hours hereafter, they are either of them, or both of them be found in the town of Providence without leave obtained, the Town Sergeant, Henry Bowen, is directed to take them into custody and unless fine be paid, to inflict on him or her or both, the corporal Punishment by law subscribed, and the same to continue so long and so often as he or she or both shall appear in town."

There was a postscript, *"Be it also resolved that the Keeper of the Gaol in Providence be requested to keep Jonathan Clarke and his wife Phebe in custody until the Town Sergeant can remove them at the expense of the Town."*

Thus the Clarkes spent the first months of their marriage driven from gaol to gaol by Henry Bowen, the man who had called Polly and Betsy his daughters.

"May 18, 1790. Expenses for moving Jonathan Clarke and his wife Phebe to North Providence. Expenses for cart, seven shillings, six pence, paid to Henry Bowen."

"June 30, 1790. Received of Henry Bowen... Jonathan Clarke and his wife Phebe with the original warrant for their removal to Boston in the Massachusetts. Constable."

And again in November: *"Received of Henry Bowen... Jonathan Clarke and his wife Phebe, with the original warrant for their Removal to Weymouth in the Massachusetts. Constable."*

The Clarkes, who left Polly and Betsy behind, were driven from North Providence across the Seekonk River to Taunton, to North Brookfield, to Boston where Clarke's daughter, also named Polly, joined them. They moved on to Weymouth and to Rutland where they lived until 1794 in a cave fifteen by twenty feet, dug into the sand of Goose Hill. There were no windows. A door led to the roof and the sole aperture, a chimney opened into the side of the hill. At the time of the contest for the estate of Madame Jumel, the Clarke's brief stay was almost forgotten. Old men prodded by Bowen's lawyers said Clarke drank too much and that Polly and Betsy lived with them. The latter at least is not true.

Traveling slowly, following rough roads and

29

wild trails, the Clarkes made their way from Rutland in Massachusetts to the Roanoke Valley in North Carolina. It is easy to see what drove them - the pursuit of Henry Bowen, the harshness of the vagrancy laws, the hopelessness of establishing themselves without credentials, the coldness of New England winters. The journey took four years. At least part of the time they traveled with a horse. It was common then for a woman to ride pillion behind a man. In fair weather, they were sometimes happy as husband and wife.

The South was as exotic as a foreign country: the red clay, the moss draped swamps, the jungles of honeysuckle, the forest of loblolly pine, the heat, the rain, poisonous snakes, chiggers, and the ticks. South of the Blue Ridge they passed great plantations where slaves worked naked in the mud flats under the whips of overseers. The Clarkes were horrified.

They were more compatible with poor whites who lived in log cabins in the woods, cultivating no more land than they needed for a crop of corn and cabbage. These were rough people. In Carolina a man could kick a stranger to death and be fined no more than a shilling. To such men New Englanders were a race apart. Even in 1798, the Clarkes were called *"dam'd Yankees."* The *"rasping whine"* in their speech gave offense and their *"reservations seemed cold and crabbly and sly."*

The Clarkes settled in Williamston, the Old Port of Entry, whose black creeks emptied into a brackish sound with an archipelago of islands. They believed they could live there without being harassed, but they were too foreign, and Clarke too conscious of himself as a gentleman to appear the savage native.

In May he paid Edward Griffin three dollars and thirty-three cents for a month's rent. In July the Clarkes went to law against their landlord, accusing him of stealing their household goods, which doubtless Griffin took, if he did, in lieu of the rent for June.

The Williamston courthouse sat on stilts in the river. To enter, the Clarkes, the Griffins and officer of the court rowed to the building, tethered their boats and climbed a ladder which the magistrates hauled up after them. No one could leave until justice was done. Strangers rarely prevailed in a local quarrel and the case was settled against the Clarkes. Jonathan was incorrigible. He appealed.

There is one more entry in the Williamston annals of the case of Clarke *vs.* Griffin. *"Case abated by the death of the plaintiffs."* Perhaps the Clarkes were murdered. It was a common solution in such quarrels. In any case, by December 1798, Phebe and Jonathan were dead.

The second paper in Madame Jumel's attic was a receipt: *"Received of Jonathan Clarke, twelve dollars in full payment of the demands of this state. Rutland, Massachusetts. 1794."*

The third paper was an inventory of Phebe's stolen goods: *"An inventory of the goods stolen from me by Edward Griffin & Company, July 4, 1798: Two skillets, an iron pot and one skirt."* Perhaps Madame kept that pathetic paper to prove that her mother, on Independence Day, in her forty-fourth year, four months before she died, went to law of her own accord. She had not then been pursued by it all her life.

31

5

"The orphaned child brought up by the overseer may
rise."
John Todd

Men no longer made their wills and settled their
affairs before taking a stage coach. In Providence in
1790, sophisticated people could face a man who had
been to Boston calmly. But the arrival and departures
of packet ships, those graceful vessels which sailed
between Providence and New York, still drew crowds
to the dock.

Betsy Bowen was fifteen, celebrated as the most
beautiful harlot in Providence, when she embarked on
such a ship to seek her fortune in New York, the new
capital, the court of the new republic. She had
redefined herself and her status in society. She would
be a seducer rather than seduced, a mistress rather than
chattel; although she was professionally exactly that - "a
movable piece of property."

Sometimes, astounded by the power of
sexuality, the adolescent ego permits itself great,
unlikely expectations; asserts itself without
moderation. Betsy's did and was divided. Knowing
from awful experience that society despises a whore,
and knowing with equal certainty that her beauty
commanded admiration she was in her own estimation,
both worthless and of great value. The split would
widen, the parameters would change, but she would
never be free of the dichotomy.

She was adept at self-deception. Her sense that
whatever she wanted was possible made her act boldly.

But she lacked balance, and her high spirits were sometimes manic. In such elation she approached New York, a city as provincial and vainglorious as herself.

The harbor was filled with ships: brigs, barks, brigantines, British frigates, French men-of-war and hundreds of lesser vessels: sloops, barges, and the boats of fishermen and green grocers.

Beyond Greenwich Village lay fields and forests. The city was crowded into the lower tip of the island where the ravages of war were still painfully visible. The port had been occupied by the British for seven years and fire had burned the whole Broad Way. Nevertheless, it was a great city. The Broad Way, where it began at Bowling Green, was seventy feet wide. The empty pedestal in the center, where a gilded statue of George III had shone in the sun, was a fitting symbol of America's transition from colony to free republic.

No one could fail to respond to New York's frenzy of patriotism. Watching the pageant designed by Charles l'Enfant to bring the three malingering states under the shelter of the Constitution, Betsy was overwhelmed. It was a pageant fit for the court of Versailles; for the Sun King.

Ten matched horses pulled a frigate called the Ship of State down the Broad Way. It was a true sea-going vessel, commanded by a commodore, manned by thirty sailors and equipped with thirty-two guns. The ship was followed by trumpeters, light-horse cavalry, cannons, and floats representing every trade and profession practiced in the United States except Betsy Bowen's. Foresters with axes were followed by farmers with oxen, tailors, bakers - whose ten bay

33

horses pulled the Federal loaf with the names of the ten ratified states sculptured into the bread. One hundred brewers pulled a float holding a pyramid of hogshead ridden by a beautiful boy in flesh-colored tights who pretended to be drinking from a silver goblet. Butchers followed a thousand pound roast bullock; who were followed by coopers, tanners, curriers, the Sons of St. Crispin,   and the heroic Society of Cincinnati. Furriers, led by a man in a white bear skin, pulled a mountain of furs with two live bears chained to a tree on top. Indians smoking tomahawk pipes marched in scarlet robes and feather bonnets.   Hatters, dress makers, wig makers, florists, cutlers with green silk aprons over steel breastplates, confectioners with a Federal cake twenty feet high were followed by stone masons pulling the Temple of Fame with thirteen pillars - ten finished and three to go. Upholsterers marched under a canopy of blue satin fringed with gold. These floats were followed by a figure of blind Justice holding gold scales, which was followed by a huge effigy of Hamilton holding the Constitution in his right hand. Bricklayers hauled the motto of their trade, *In God is Our Trust* spelled in open brickwork. Cabinet makers with a great cradle for the infant nation, musicians pulling Apollo playing a lyre, paper stainers, civil engineers, shipwrights pulling Noah's Ark,   one-hundred-and-twenty   blacksmiths,   ship joiners, boat builders carrying pine branches, forty-one riggers rigging a ship with a banner saying, *Rig Me Neat and Join Me to the Federal Fleet*, were followed by goldsmiths, silversmiths, saddlers, whip makers, and a detachment of artillery.   These were followed by brush makers, chocolate makers, tobacconists, dyers, tallow candlers, coppersmiths, and tin workers pulling the Federal Tin House with the motto, *When Three More Pillars Rise, Our Union Will The World Surprise*, which were followed by merchants, clergymen, physicians, scholars, gentlemen and strangers. And when the Ship of State passed the Federal building firing its thirty-two guns, all the ships in the harbor answered.

Then the first Congress met in Federal Hall and unanimously voted to make Washington the first President of the United States with Adams as his Vice President. Only then, a messenger rode to Mt. Vernon to tell the General the news.

Washington waited a whole day before beginning his triumphal march. It took him seven days to cover the two-hundred-and-thirty miles between Mt. Vernon and New York. In every village along the way, he rode under triumphal arches and down avenues of laurels. In village after village, he was preceded by flower girls like a bridegroom. At Elizabeth Point he boarded a barge with a red pavilion hung with garlands, manned by thirteen ship's captains dressed in white uniforms. The General's float was followed by every other vessel which had a berth along the shore. As Washington's barge slipped between New Jersey and Staten Island, it was met by hundreds of other boats which saluted him as he passed. Gentlemen sang odes to him. Ladies shouted poems. Bands played, not deterred by the deafening din of huzzahs and the roar of artillery.

At Murphy's Wharf Washington stepped ashore onto a red carpet. He strode through the joyous celebrating throngs, past buildings decorated in every way ingenuity could invent with the name *Washington*, while flowers fell like snow, and the successive raising of hats rolled like the motion of a field of grain in the wind, and every house he passed was decorated with garlands and evergreen branches; on to his own house on Cherry Street, and out again to dine with Governor Clinton. That evening every house in the City, except those where Quakers lived, was illuminated; so that windows *"seemed like living paintings."*

The General took his oath of office on the balcony of Federal Hall. He wore a brown suit. Lace fell over his bosom and covered his huge hands. As he kissed the Bible, a universal shout went up, as if *"every mind was filled with one idea and every heart swelled with one emotion."* And as if the joy were universal, England too made the thirtieth day of April a day of Thanksgiving. George III had recovered his mind.

That contagion of joy and delirium of patriotism made the act of love, even for a whore like Betsy, an integral part of the celebration - as soldiers and women in a liberated town are drawn to one another in carnal elation, or as strangers embrace on the occasion of a great victory or longed for armistice. In the new capital, men and women who would become immortal passed each other as if they were merely human. Thomas Jefferson and John Paul Jones lived on the Broad Way. James Madison and John Hancock on Smith Street. Washington and Franklin on Cherry. Burr on Nassau. Hamilton on Wall. Adams at Richmond Hill. Tom Paine, James Monroe, even Horatio Nelson lived in the City then.

Washington took no pleasure in the pomp of his circumstances. Witnesses said he looked pale, even cadaverous. The set of his face was habitually so sober

36

that it passed for melancholy. Except at the theater, when he enjoyed what passed for ribald comedy, no one every saw him smile.

The silent levees he presided over on Tuesday and Friday nights were ordeals for him as well as his guests. The President thumped endlessly on the edge of the table with his fork. Because these levees were open to anyone with proper clothes, it was then that Betsy renewed her acquaintance with the great man.

Mercifully, by summer a malignant carbuncle forced the President to lie on his side for six weeks, thus curtailing his social activities.

If there were no legitimate majesty, it was not for want of pretending. Those wealthy Tories who had openly sympathized with George III, became the arbiters of society. French visitors were astonished at the capital's luxury and ostentation. Jefferson was appalled. Hamilton and his wife entertained lavishly, and in his own home he spoke openly about his loathing for *"that poison, democracy."* General Knox gave a formal dinner every other week. Because he and his lady together weighed more than five hundred pounds, they were called the greatest couple in New York.

The pace was giddy, and for hangers on, the cost of living was horrifying. *"Luxury is already forming in this city a very dangerous class of men, namely bachelors,"* warned a minister, *"for the extravagance of our women makes men dread marriage."* In his journal of gossip, Fenno wrote that the new fashion of sleeves above the elbows made ladies look like washerwomen; that bells tolling for funerals kept Congress from concentrating; that Hamilton was seen kissing a coquette and Burr handing a courtesan to her carriage.

37

Since there were as yet no class distinctions and anyone who wanted to play the game was welcome, Betsy knew the men she would say had loved her: Washington, Patrick Henry, Hamilton and Burr. Hamilton and Burr did indeed sleep with her. She said the aged Franklin called her his *"faerie queen."*

She lived beyond her means and Aaron Burr paid her debts, bought her release from New York's wretched Bridewell. He at least had shown her affection. He advised her to go back to Providence.

6

"The law once was that an illegitimate son was the son of nobody, although it is an historical fact that the greatest men who have ever blessed or cursed the earth found themselves ushered into this state of existence as illegitimate. And in all cases one may quote the lines of Robert Burns, '*A man's a man for all 'that'.*"
Opening speech for the plaintiff, George Washington Bowen.

Old Hull remembered that Betsy walked the streets of Providence with her sister Polly and half-sister Lavinia; and that men took them to Mother Ballous as they had before. "*I used to see Betsy around so much I can't tell you,*" Hull told the court. "*I saw her flirting around the streets at a great rate and everyone talking about it and about her being back. I can remembers her looks like it was now. She was tall and slim and very pretty.*"

Other witnesses confirmed Hull's memory. "*Everyone knew what she did,*" said an old mariner. "*She was celebrated because she was the handsomest girl in Providence.*"

"*She was a loose woman, but likely looking, I guess,*" said Catherine Williams. "*I used to see her laughing with the girls as she walked down Cheapside. That was the great promenade for ladies of her sort - painted women.*"

In the spring of 1794, when Betsy found she was pregnant, she did not, as other women did, withdraw from view. All that long summer and fall she flaunted her belly, while Old Mother Ballou told everyone that the father was a person of high blood. *"All the talk was she was going to have it by a rich man."* Hull told the court. *"People used to talk about her shape and we boys always used to laugh at her because she was so large. In those days, we boys always used to laugh at them and call them barrel-belly."*

But the manic temperament has a darker side, when all senses impact making the psyche so dense that nothing can enter and nothing can leave. Then Betsy could hide at Mother Ballou's, in an empty room or in the gambreled attic; lying on a corn husk mattress or in a nest of blankets; too passive to weep; letting memories drift and merge in alternative patterns of despair.

Such grief can be relieved by a raging tantrum. Betsy's tongue was profane enough. But on the streets of Providence, until her child was due, she maintained the image of a woman who could neither be humiliated nor made afraid.

She was safe at the Ballous. They owned an old house in the oldest part of town, near the old grist mill, the New Gaol and the Muddy Dock Tavern. The house backed the river and on the river path a man could come in without being seen. Privacy was an advantage, because Freelove not only rented rooms to prostitutes, she treated venereal disease, which no respectable physician would even attempt.

No one threatened the Ballous. Freelove, nee Whipple, was not a vagrant to be warned out. The Council met her at her father's tavern and made such decisions after they had wined and dined. In truth, in considering Freelove's, or any other brothel, the Council was not concerned with morality. In consideration of their pocketbooks, the fathers brought

40

different sides of their consciences to bear. The practical magistrate saw Mother Ballou's as a necessary evil, but in judging a woman without a man's support, who might become a charge of the town, the same magistrate became a righteous Puritan. Reuben's reputation protected his wife. He had been a Major in the Revolution. He practiced an honest trade, and he had married Freelove in the great stone Baptist Church. But when witnesses spoke of him, he was remembered only as a florid, fleshy man who drank too much.

When they spoke of Freelove, they were more voluble. *"People were afraid of her,"* said an old woman. *"So when they talked to her face, they called her Missus; but behind her back it was Old Mother Ballou. We used to hear her hollering in the streets. She hollered her head off when she was put in gaol - it wasn't but a hundred yards from her house, but aslant. She would call out and talk back and forth with the men in her house so you could hear every word. And she was in gaol for being the receiver of stolen goods."*

On the ninth of October, 1794, Freelove helped Betsy deliver a baby boy. She was a skilled midwife, mixing magic and practical help with that empathy which does not confuse labor with a doctor's efforts. Certainly the women she delivered did not die of infection as they did in the infamous lying-in hospitals of New York and Philadelphia.

Her magic was traditional, an ax under the bed to cut pain; catnip and alder tea mixed the ground ivy, *"not to work around the heart, but to make a woman cramp and jump."* She smoothed the birth canal with egg whites and kneaded Betsy's contracted belly. When the baby was born and the umbilical cut, she scorched a piece of flannel and pulled the baby's cord through a

41

button hole, buttoning and protecting his belly before she bound it with a band. Finally, she gave the child to Betsy to let him suck. Thus, she allowed Betsy, however briefly, bonding moments of awe and delight.

But Betsy was not allowed to nurse her baby. Three days later, when her breasts were blue-veined and swollen, Freelove made Betsy splash a dollop of milk on the hot bricks of the fireplace to hiss and disappear; conjuring the drying of her milk.

In the absence of Phebe, Betsy was comforted by Freelove's familiar bawdy presence. The young whore was proud of her son. *"I used to carry water crackers to the Ballou's two or three times a week,"* said Daniel Hull. *"And when Betsy called me in, she was sitting up in bed with the plaintiff in her arms and she said would I like to look at her fat little baby. Says she, 'How do you like the look of him?' Says I, 'He's a likely boy.'*

Says she, 'I want you to buy some candy.' I can't remember how many coppers she gave me. I used to see her every day after she got well."

Hull didn't visit Betsy to see her baby or take her coppers. *"I used to go there to play with her monkey, you see. I always carried him something to eat. But after it bit me, I didn't go with him for a time."* But he went back. *"Then after she got well,* Hull said. *"I used to see her carrying it around in her arms and nursing it out of a kind of bottle. I guess she didn't give no milk. I judge she was from fifteen to eighteen, somewhere between there."*

Reuben Ballou recorded the birth in the only book he had, a volume published in Pope's Head Alley in 1599, *The First Part of the Raigne of Henri the III Extended to the End of the First Year of His Raigne.* In that precious book, he wrote, *"George Washington*

Bowen, born of Eliza (so she began to call herself) Bowen at my house in Providence, this ninth of October, 1794. Reuben Ballou."

For powerful reasons neither Reuben, Freelove nor Betsy ever revealed the name of *"the rich man of high degree and high blood"* who fathered the baby. Lavinia would testify that Reuben suggested the name. Probably in retrospect his old commander seemed god-like. In any case, Reuben dealt with the agent of the boy's father, and accepted money for the child's support.

Eliza left her baby with Freelove, to give him away as her mother had given her children away; her firstborn, John Thomas, and her daughter Lavinia.

"It was in the warm weather she left him," said Hull. If the weather was warm, George must have been six months old. Eliza had changed him, swaddled him, bottled him, comforted him with sugar teats, rubbed his sore gums with rum. When she left him he was responsive, gurgled and crowed to see her; and when she held him under the arms, he danced on her lap. He could almost sit up alone, leaning forward on his arms.

Eliza did not find it easy to abandon her son, except as it is easy to act when there is no alternative. She gathered her power, resolved that when she could, she would come back and acknowledge him. Then, assuming that cheerfulness which makes action possible, she sailed again to New York. *"When she left on the packet,"* said Hull, *"the baby was in there with Missus Ballou."*

7

"From the bottom to the top without a ladder or a
rope. Sweep ho!"
Street cry

The father of Eliza's baby sent her away under
the protection of a captain named Mason, a situation
Mason's wife found tolerable. But, Eliza did not cling
to people who knew her as Betsy Bowen. Most of the
time she believed she could make men as dependent on
her favors as she had been on theirs. Such buoyant
vanity was an enormous asset, except when it
overwhelmed her judgment, and became dangerous.
She plied her trade in an unsavory district called the
Holy Lane, after a similar maze of brothels and taverns
in London. Of necessity, her adventures were
sometimes sordid and frightening.

Everywhere in New York, in the streets and
taverns and coffee houses, men argued about the
French Revolution. Like other whores, Eliza wore the
politics she knew so little about, around her neck - a
red velvet ribbon in morbid tribute to the guillotined
King of France. But she went further and called herself
Eliza Capet. Such a name and ribbon were deliberate
provocation. The late king was rudely called by his
family name. *Capet is Kaput* said a New York
newspaper.

Like her son, who came to believe that his
father was General Washington, Eliza had reason to
mystify her birth, emotional as well as practical need to
obliterate Providence, to be born again in the court of
France. Capet was a frivolous nom de querre, but it

44

sprang from a powerful need.

The story she told was equivocal. She said she was born on a French frigate carrying soldiers to Santo Domingo. Her English mother was noble. Implied but never explicit was the suggestion that her mother fled on a French ship with French soldiers because she carried the French king's child. The story, never examined, never articulated, never lost its power.

Eliza told men that her mother died in childbirth and was buried at sea. The captain nurtured the infant until a storm blew his vessel into the harbor of Newport (so little did Eliza know of the distance between Santo Domingo and Rhode Island). In Newport, Widow Thompson adopted Eliza and raised her as her own. When the widow died, Eliza sailed to New York, where - this was the common evasion of streetwalkers - she said she earned her living as a seamstress.

She could not tell this story to Aaron Burr. But when he saw her again, her resiliency must have seemed piquant and passed for gallantry - the virtue he valued above all others. For Burr it was a matter of honor to make the most of pleasure, the least of sorrow and to bound up lightly after a fall. Again his relationship with Eliza was casual and carnal, but this time he kept her in a house on Chatham Street.

After the death of his wife, Burr withheld his love from everyone except his daughter Theodosia, whom he made, in all but sex, the surrogate of his beloved wife. Most of the women be bedded and left forgave him. Many retained his friendship. He was Eliza's counterpart, l'homme fatale. He was forty-two, in loco parentis, her father, mentor and demon lover.

Eliza's description of Burr (from an article in

the <u>New York Times</u> attributed to Madame at the time of her death) is not less glowing for being written in old age: *Colonel Burr, in the heyday of his youth, as he appeared to me," she wrote, "was the perfection of manhood personified. He was beneath the common size of men, only five feet-and-a-half high, but his figure and form had been fashioned in the Model of the Graces. Petit as he comparatively was, he had a martial appearance, and displayed in all his movements those accomplishments which are only acquired in the boudoir of the Graces. In a word, he was a model of Mars and Apollo.*

His eye was of the deepest black and sparkled with incomparable brilliance when he smiled. But, if enraged, its power was absolutely terrible. Into whatever female society he chance by the fortunes of war or the vicissitudes of private life to be cast, he conquered all hearts without an effort; and until he became deeply involved in the cares of state and the vexations of the political arena, I do not believe a female capable of the gentle emotion of love, ever looked on him without loving him. Wherever he went he was petted and caressed by our sex, and hundreds vied with each other in a continuous struggle to offer him some testimonial of their adulation. And yet, I do not believe that any female ever had caused to complain of his seductive wiles, perfidy or injustice."

That this extraordinary tribute was based on more than the vanity of Madame Jumel is born out by the journal of a young man, who after an evening with Burr wrote in similar terms. *"Burr is spare, meager of form, but of elegant symmetry. His complexion fair, transparent. His dress fashionable and rich, but not flashy. He is commanding, his aspect mild, firm, luminous and impressive... His eyes are dark hazel and from the shade of his projecting brows, appear black. They glow with the ardor of venereal fire and scintillate with the most tremendous sensibility. They roll with the celerity and frenzy of poetic fervor, and beam with the most vivid and piercing eye of genius. His mouth is large, his voice manly, clear and melodious. His radiance dazzles the sight...*

He seems passionately fond of female society. To the ladies he is all attention, all devotion. In conversation he gazes on them with rapture, and when he addresses them, it is with that je sais quois, those disarming looks, that soft, sweet insinuating eloquence which takes the heart captive."

Part of Burr's charm was his belief that the minds of men and women were equal; his conviction that women should be educated as well as men, and in the same subjects.

He taught Eliza something of clothes and etiquette, to play whist, to distinguish the various virtues of horses and carriages. He could not fail to appreciate that she had learned to read and write, even to speak French. He added the names, Voltaire, Rousseau and Chesterfield to her smattering of worldliness. All her life, Eliza was proud of her marksmanship. She practiced with pistols with Burr on the shaded terrace behind Richmond Hill.

His estate encompassed most of Greenwich Village. The house had been built by Lord Jeffery Amherst. Adams lived there as Vice President; his wife Abigail called it the most beautiful estate in America. *"The noble Hudson with its vessels...the fertile Jerseys...their verdure and golden harvests...the ancient trees...a grove of pines fit for contemplation."* Impressed her.

Farms and boats did not impress Eliza. But the

mansion with its pillars and porticos did; and the grace of Burr's household; the loyalty of his twenty slaves, did not fail to move her.

In the beginning, before Eliza was established on Chatham Street, Burr took her to the majestic Morris Mansion on Harlem Heights. No site in Manhattan commanded such a view. From the balcony the lovers could see the Harlem, the East and the Hudson Rivers, with all of Manhattan below. The lovely haziness of Eastchester and New Jersey spread out on either hand. The house had been Washington's Headquarters after his retreat from the city; and Burr had lived there as one of the General's military family. When Burr brought Eliza to the Heights, it was a place of assignation, an inn, the first stop on the Albany Post Road.

This was the house Eliza would rule as Madame Jumel, the house she would share with Burr as man and wife. But that she should own so great a mansion, or that Burr should marry a prostitute was, at that time, farther from either of their minds than the moon from the earth.

The house represented Burr's past. He shared his memories with Eliza, showed her the room where the British courier told them that Nathan Hale had been executed. He confided more. Hale had been hanged for arson while New York burned. Washington, who had asked permission to burn the city and had been forbidden to do so by Congress, watched the great fire stoically and as stoically received the news of Hale's heroic death.

Burr showed Eliza the huge octagonal Chamber for Courts Martial, where Mary Morris' green wall paper still hung on buckram panels. Lieutenant

Leffingwell had been condemned to death for cowardice there; and a common solider sentenced to forty lashes for singing *God Save the King.* Madame Jumel would line the room with mirrors.

Burr took Eliza up the back stairs (where he had conducted two sachems of the Cayuga National who came to pledge their loyalty). He showed her the core of their Headquarters. This was Washington's office, this his map room, this his bedroom. Hamilton slept there; I slept here. They explored the old battlements which infringed on the gardens. Eliza reminded Burr of Washington's familiarity at the home of the man she now called her father, Major Reuben Ballou.

Burr's military exploits were heroic and often extraordinary. But he honored himself too much as a soldier to speak of them lightly. He did not tell Eliza about his part in the retreat to the Mansion. Burr brought up the rear which in such circumstances is as dangerous as leading an attack. At Grand Street, he found Washington's great friend, Colonel Knox, cowering in a sod hut with a brigade of frightened men, without food or water or ammunition. *"Come with me now, or die like dogs tomorrow,"* Burr said. All that night the reluctant Knox and his even more reluctant men straggled through the fragrant countryside; while Burr rode coolly from front to rear, inspiring the demoralized recruits with his composure.

Pointedly Washington failed to commend Burr; and pointedly he failed to recommend him for the rank of Colonel, although he soon conferred that rank on Hamilton who did not fight until the battle of Yorktown (when he hid behind the great bulk of General Knox). Washington loved Hamilton like a son, but Burr's pride irritated him. Thus in the Morris

49

Mansion, the rivalry between the two young men was exacerbated by Washington.

By the time Burr brought Eliza to the Mansion, the old rivals were famous lawyers. They had paced each other step by step, scrupulously maintaining the appearance of friendship; and when Hamilton challenged James Monroe to a duel, Burr successfully acted as mediator.

They were always politically opposed. Burr had no scruples about using his mistress as a political spy. *"He thrust Eliza into Hamilton's bed,"* said Colonel Craft, Burr's partner in law.

It pleased Eliza to prove she could seduce whom she pleased, or whom it pleased Burr that she please. But she was also hurt. If he loved her he would have barred others from her bed. Nevertheless, Hamilton was attractive. He wielded power; and in his bed, if only for the moment, Eliza held his power in her power, the common satisfaction of a prostitute.

"She stole the Adams letter and gave it to Burr," said Colonel Craft. The letter was pivotal in the election of 1796. It made Adams President and paved the way for the election of Jefferson and Burr. Eliza never knew its significance. She never boasted about it. She was as apolitical as she was amoral, incapable of committing herself to any cause larger than herself. Had she considered her sympathies, she would have preferred Hamilton's ideal of monarchy to Burr's concept of democracy. Kings and courts were more compatible with her fantasies.

The letter Eliza stole: A LETTER CONCERNING THE PUBLIC CONDUCT AND PRIVATE CHARACTER OF JOHN ADAMS, was meant to be secretly circulated among Hamilton's

Federalist friends. In scandalous, vituperative terms Hamilton betrayed Adams (whom he publicly supported) as well as the Federalist Party to which he belonged; hoping by thus undoing Adams, to promote his own candidacy. In another, less widely circulated letter, Hamilton wrote more wildly. *"If Adams is elected, a Revolution will ensue, and I will either loose my head, or be at the head of a triumphant army."*

The matter was inflammatory. Burr published the letter in every newspaper in the United States. Neither the Federalists nor Hamilton ever recovered. Until the end of his life, Adams could not say Hamilton's name without the qualifying word *'bastard.'* Hamilton, retiring from politics, bought property on Harlem Heights where he took Voltaire's advice and cultivated his garden.

"Then" Burr's seminal biography, James Parton, would write, *"Then the Old Things in this country really passed away. Then rose the Conquering Democratic Party. Then America became America."* One may thank Eliza.

Eliza never believed Burr was faithful. He was not; nor was she the only woman he made love to and used as a spy. Mary Hassals, who loved him dearly, wrote regularly from Santo Domingo. Eliza began to see other men, and Colonel Craft spoke of her house on Chatham Street as notorious.

Burr was a man of many parts, projects and plots. In the dullest times he traveled between Albany, New York, Philadelphia, Washington and Charleston. Heartache did not make Eliza less able to accept the inevitable. When Burr abandoned her, she replaced him with a French merchant, Captain Jacques de la Croix, in whose less dazzling company, she felt at ease.

8

"In order to know what is due her, to know what
power she has, a woman must live for six months in
Paris."
"Napoleon"

Eliza traveled with de la Croix and when she
was twenty-two, she posed for Charles Balthazaar
Julien Ferret St. Memin as Madame de la Croix.
Presumably, sailing between New York and France, a
man without roots, de la Croix could afford to call a
woman his wife when she was not. Eliza responded
demurely. In St. Memin's portrait she is modestly
dressed, wearing a chemise l'anglais with a fichu at her
throat becoming her mock status as matron.

St. Memin's portraits conferred respectability on
most of his sitters. In a country without nobility, they
would in time, assume the importance of a coronet. St.
Memin was a refugee from Santo Domingo, a
mathematician, an inventor, an archaeologist; a genius,
who finding himself unemployed in the new Republic,
turned to portraiture. He was a skilled draftsman. But
he prospered because, in addition to a conté-crayon
profile on pink paper, he made thirteen engravings on a
reducing machine of his own invention. Of these he
kept one for his personal records, leaving his sitter with
the elegant equivalent of a dozen photographs. In an
age when only a rich man could afford to sit for a
competent painter, his portraits were an undoubted
bargain.

St. Memin never flattered a sitter. Sometimes
he verged on caricature. He belittled Eliza's beauty.

But even in profile, the sculpture of her eye sockets, the fullness of her lids, the arch of her brows is startlingly beautiful. Her hair is long, Except for the pin which catches up the sides, the mass falls down her back. Her nose is pert. Her smile insouciant and sweet. The portraits of great courtesans, the mistresses of kings, often suggest the same sweet amiability. (Madame's temperament was not, however, amiable.) St. Memin always dated his engravings. On Eliza's he wrote, Mde. de la Croix, 1797.

She visited France with her merchant captain. Crossing the Atlantic was always dangerous but crossing France was more frightening. At Le Havre or Bordeaux or Marseilles, wherever their vessel made port, customs officials swarmed over the ship demanding bribes. In every port beggars made the streets unsafe; brigands terrorized the roads. Five men rode shotgun on the roofs of public stages, and as these coaches rolled through shuttered villages, redolent of dung and dust, every visitor was struck by the fact that able-bodied men had vanished, leaving only old women to till the fields.

Paris was still Medieval, not yet the city of grace and space. Emigres creeping back appraised each other like strangers meeting on a desert island. When they crossed La Place de La Revolution, their eyes avoided the spot where the guillotine had been.

Eliza saw Paris as a festival, a city where romance was celebrated without stint or stop. *"Balls and spectacles have replaced Revolutionary committees,"* a friend wrote St. Méry. *"There are the same fops and loose women, the same elaborate dressing... You know how the women of the court, the prostitutes appeared wherever they could show off or have pleasure? How they drew in their wake the giddy fools whose happiness was pleasing fashionable women? Only the individuals have changed. The women of the court have been replaced by the nouveau riches and in their train are the prostitutes who fight with them for the wherewithal of luxury and extravagance... the wanton swarm called merveileux, who talk politics as they dance, sigh for royalty as they eat ices and yawn at fireworks."*

There were two thousand dance halls in Paris. The Palais d'Elysee had been the first. Now they were everywhere; in a Jesuit novitiate, in the Carmelite convent...Over the gates of St. Surplice, where the sacristy steps were stained with the blood of murdered priests, a pink gauze transparency advertised Le Palais de Zephre. Parisians *"danced to put those pale lost lilies out of mind,"* the fleur de lis of beheaded Bourbons. Conventions were inverted. A whore was the social arbiter of Paris. In a parody of Roman drapery she and her friends wore gowns so thin that the circlets of their garters gleamed through the gauze, the shyer women wore *"apron handkerchiefs"* to hide their pubic hair.

Eliza, who sat so demurely for St. Memin, who called herself Madame de la Croix, belonged by nature with the merveileux. Her delight in this city where sexuality and beauty were glorified, offended her respectable lover. He saw the dancing and copulating of the merveileux as repellent as the convulsions of headless chickens.

With or without de la Croix's permission (any American could ask for an invitation) Eliza was presented to the First Consul. Napoleon's intimacies with women were frequent and casual. If he found a woman attractive, he sent his equerry to tell her when to expect his carriage. Most women were honored and

54

happy to be escorted to the Tuileries, led to the Consul's bedroom. When he was not preoccupied, he was an endearing lover.

"He came over to me with that enchanting smile which was his alone," wrote Mlle. George after her assignation. *"He took me by the hand and sat me down on that enormous divan, then lifted my veil and threw it to the floor... Little by little he undid all my clothes. He played the role of femme de chambre with such gaiety, grace and decency that one simply had to yield. How could one fail to be fascinated by that man and attracted to him? He played the little boy and child to please me. He was no longer the Consul; he was a man in love. But it was a love in which violence and roughness had no part.*

He was laughing and playing with me, making me run after him. To avoid getting caught, he climbed up on the ladder he used to get books from the shelves. Since the ladder was on rollers and very light, I pushed it the entire length of the study while he laughed at me. 'You're going to hurt yourself. Stop, or I'll get angry'."

On the fourth night, he stuffed a bundle of bank notes in my bosom, 40,000 francs, saying 'I don't want my darling to lack money when I'm away'."

Jacques de la Croix abruptly ended his affair with Eliza. He had the goodness to leave her in New York; and having no choice, she plied her trade again in the Holy Land. This time she called herself Eliza Brown, after one, or perhaps four, of the famous merchants of Providence.

9

"The grand blanc is generous, hospitable and
magnificent."
Mary Hassals

All Eliza's adventures had been prologue,
preparation for the real drama, her marriage to Stephen
Jumel. He was French, a grand blanc, part owner of a
coffee plantation in Santo Domingo, until Toussaint's
Revolution made him a refugee. He was forty-two
when Eliza met him in New York, a merchant prince,
an owner of ships, and importer of wines. He was
handsome, single and wealthy, popular with his peers.

He had been in love. The erotic climate of
Santo Domingo was all pervasive. It made Mary
Hassals (Burr's agent) sick with longing: *"O my friend,
what a delightful existence,"* she wrote, *"to pass life away
in the arms of voluptuous indulgence...Libertinism is
without restraint. The faux-pas of a lady is so much a
matter of course, that she who has only one lover and
retains him long in her chains is a model of constancy and
discretion. In three days a love affair is begun, finished
and forgotten. The first day is for declaration, the second
is the day of triumph - if it is delayed so long - and the
third is for adieu."*

In Santo Domingo Stephen ruled his slaves like
a sovereign. He had been his own overseer; rising
before daylight to go to his fields, stopping for
breakfast at eleven, sleeping away the afternoon,
gaming and drinking away the night. Rum, he and his
fellows half-believed, gave them immunity to malaria
and yellow fever.

"But in this abode of luxurious ease," wrote Mary Hassals, *"vices reign at which humanity must shudder,"* Slavery in Santo Domingo was more cruel than in America. Its savagery, rooted in sadism and grounded in boredom, horrified Mary and she wrote Burr about it at length.

Inevitably the hatred engendered by countless atrocities against black slaves could not be contained. In the course of the Revolution, led by Toussaint l'Ouverture, hundreds of French planters and their families were tortured and killed. Jumel escaped in 1791 at the time of the great exodus. Surrounded by two black armies, the Commissioner at Le Cap surrendered. Le Cap, 'little Paris of West,' was set on fire. Hundreds of whites who had come to the city for the protection of its garrison, battled for a place on the quays. While the retreating army fought in the flames and crashing timbers. French frigates and American merchant vessels took colonials and soldiers aboard as quickly as they could. But scores were drowned as life boats were overturned by struggling men.

Jumel was taken aboard an American slaver bound for St. Helena, on its rounds to the Guinea Coast of Africa. From the safety of the ship, Jumel and his fellows stared back at the ruined harbor. *"A luminous haze obscured the sun. In the mountains clouds of smoke with tongues of fire, distant plantations at that moment in flames, looked like infant volcanoes,"* a survivor wrote. *"But the most dreadful aspect of the scene was the airborne burning cane, now dancing over the harbor, now over its ships,"* In the course of its triangular rounds, Jumel's slaver carried him to New York, for which he paid either all he had or nothing, according to the captain's political sympathy.

He was warmly welcomed. New York was almost as full of Frenchmen as Providence had been during the War. On Vesy Street alone, three hundred emigres were fed and housed at the expense of the City. And on the Fourth of July 1794, watching a parade pass Federal Hall, Jumel heard La Marseillaise drown out Yankee Doodle.

With the help of American friends, and with capitol loaned by his family in Bordeaux, Jumel was soon established as an importer of wine and other liquors. As he began to make money, he was given an introduction at the Tontine and a desk in the counting house of Benjamin Desorby. His business prospered. By the time he fell in love with Eliza Brown, nee Bowen, he was the wealthy head of Jumel and Desorby, with offices on Stone Street.

The life of a grand blanc in Santo Domingo had not corrupted Jumel's innate decency. He was a model of constancy in love, and affability in business. Every account speaks of his sweet nature. *"He is as fine and noble hearted a Frenchman as ever lived,"* wrote William Barret. *"Stephen Jumel was large, genial, soft-spoken and handsome,"* wrote Burr's partner, Colonel Craft. Both men told the story of the cartman's horse to illustrate Jumel's charm and benevolence. The horse had slipped on icy cobblestones and a pipe of brandy had fallen and split apart. Jumel joined the men who gathered to express their sympathy, to comfort the poor man whose horse was useless and who had to pay his employer for the spilled brandy. *"Poor fellow,"* said one. *"What a pity,"* said another. Jumel doffed his hat. *"Aha! You all peety, eh? How much you peety? I peety ten dollar."* He put ten dollars in his hat and passed it among the crowd. Thus he collected over a hundred and fifty dollars for the cartman of his rival, M. Juhel, with whom in billing, he was often confused.

Like all new lovers Eliza and Stephen had little need for friends. The privacy of New York's public places was their pleasure, and the city a theater for courtship. They could sit under the lemon trees at Brandon's Tea House, watch sky rockets from the green booths at the Vauxhall. They could dine at the City Hotel or in the Belevedere's octagonal dining room, or at the Fraunces Tavern where Washington found his famous chef, at the Raleigh with its shaded lawns or at Michael Little's where Frenchmen met to enjoy their native cooking. Testing her memory as one tests an aching tooth, Eliza drove with Jumel to Harlem Heights and the Morris Mansion where she and Burr had made love.

The homes of merchants like Jumel, their counting houses and cafes, the Tontine, the Fly Market, the East India Company, the slave market, the stock exchange and Tammany Hall were crowded in the area known as the Battery. The city had spread west from its origins, from the wharves and slips of the East River (where the great pageant's Ship of State lay rotting in dry dock) to the river called North or Hudson. The docks were raucous with activity. Vessels unloaded spices, camphor, and silk from China; coffee, rum, slaves and sugar from the Indies. They loaded cargoes of lumber, leather, flour and fish. The waterfront was loud with street cries, sea chanteys, hammering shipwrights, screeching gulls. It stank of garbage and rotting fish, tide flats, cargo and tar. Scavenger pigs ran in packs through narrow lanes, and soliciting prostitutes strolled arm in arm. This was the province of Stephen Jumel. Eliza would never walk there again, at least without complaining that no lady should be asked to do so.

Jumel and Desorby owned or had interest in a fleet of ships; brigs, barks, schooners. Of these Jumel owned outright the bark Eliza and the brig Stephen. The business of the port was complex as the interests of importers and exporters; the owners of warehouses and ships coincided. The House of Jumel & Desorby bought and sold goods as diverse as bullets and gauze. But Jumel made his fortune as a wine merchant. His advertisements are curious:

WINES: Maderia, Sherry, Tenneriffe, Malagra,
Fayal Port & Claret.
BRANDY: Cognac, Spanish, Cette, Peach &
Country.
CORDIALS: York Rum, All Fours, Soughton Bitters,
Metheglin, Cherry Bounce, Cherry Brandy, Raspberry,
Liquor d'Or, Creme de Coffe, Anisette, Penny Royal,
Brown, Wintergreen, Mint, Aqua Mirables, Noyeau, Rosa
Solis, Mount Peliever, Rattifa, Citron, Cinnamon, Ladies
Comfort, Orange, Life of Man, Distilled Life of Man.
SPIRITS: Jamaica, Antigua, St. Croix, West Indies Island,
New England.
GIN: Holland, York, Old Irish, Old Shrub, Cider
Spirits, Alcohol, High Wines, Spirits of Wine & Iron
Liquor for dressing Leather.

The Tontine was the great clearing house of marine information, where the names of all vessels were posted as they entered or cleared the port; their owners, captains, cargoes, ports of call and sail. Much of the independent business of the city was conducted there in its offices. John Jacob Astor, thick and porcine, sat in the Tontine all day, washing raw fish down with red wine, talking furs and buying land, piece by piece - building his empire as the great landlord of Manhattan. This was Jumel's second home, the club where his political opinions were honed, and his torn loyalties appeased by his profits.

Every question of national interest was judged in the context of the war between England and France, the Coalition of Kings against the Emperor Napoleon. The Tontine merchants were bound to English banks, but their hearts belonged to France. A liberty cap flew over the Stars and Stripes on their mast; and every victory of Napoleon was celebrated with pealing bells and roaring cannon. More cannons were fired in New York to celebrate the victory of Amsterdam, than were fired in the battle of Amsterdam, or so it was reported.

Meanwhile, both France and England commandeered American ships and impressed their sailors. John Adams placed his infant navy at the disposal of Toussaint l'Ouverture in Santo Domingo. This undeclared war which lasted three years, cost America one vessel and France eighty-seven. Jumel and his fellows might quarrel about national honor, but they resisted every embargo or restriction of trade. In spite of, or because of the war at sea, they prospered. If one vessel in three reached its destination, Jumel was content, for the value of its cargo had tripled.

Jumel loved Eliza deeply, but he was a merchant, not a gallant. His thoughts were usually in the counting house where his energies and moneys were engaged.

10

"Conscience has no more to do with gallantry than it
has with politics."
Richard Brinsley Sheriden

Only one witness, testifying in the case of
George Washington Bowen *vs.* Nelson Chase,
remembered Eliza as the mistress of Stephen Jumel.
But the old sailor omitted no essential. Jumel was an
indulgent lover; and Eliza, once she was established in
his yellow brick house on Pearl Street, was restless.

"O daily I saw her when I was ashore," Anthony
Fountain told the Court. *"Daily for four or five years I
saw her exhibiting herself. I was a young man and I took
notice of such things, for she was a very pretty lady indeed,
full chested and fine looking. She used to sit in the
window exhibiting herself, usually in a white muslin dress.
And her arms and bosom were bare. I used to bow to her.
I didn't know her name at first, but others did. She was
known by the name of Eliza Brown. The first time I had
to speak to her, there was a beautiful carriage standing by
the door, a very beautiful carriage. It was the finest
carriage I ever saw. And there was a pair of horses and a
coachman, a white man in livery, holding the reins in his
hands. Then she came out and said it was the present of M.
Jumel who was a merchant prince, one of the elite of the
city.*

'It's a very handsome present,' she said.

'Yes, Ma'am,' I said, 'it is'."

It did not occur to Anthony Fountain that
Eliza exhibited herself because she had no other occupation, or that she spoke to a passing sailor because

she was at ease with men like himself. Fountain made no moral judgment; but it was not the custom in New York in 1800 for a man to live openly with his mistress.

Having been excluded from the larger world of men, New York matrons were stern arbiters of virtue. They regulated schemes of benevolence, frightened clergymen, dispensed hospitality and punished women like Eliza, whose offense was particularly outrageous because she flaunted her position as Jumel's mistress without a shred of hypocrisy.

Her naked arms and bosom, her carriage (designed by the famous Abraham Quick), were affronts to virtuous women; who not only excluded Eliza from their own innocuous pastimes, their charities, whist parties and assemblies, but because she was conspicuous, made her feel invisible. They averted their eyes from her person, refused to pass her door, and withdrew to a curtained window whenever her carriage appeared. For Eliza, flouting convention in the most offensive way possible, consulting their husbands in their homes on matters concerning Stephen's business.

She involved herself in her lover's affairs, made herself cognizant in all his dealing, but she was less welcome at the Tontine or in the counting house of his fellow merchants, than in the homes of their wives.

Thus having achieved all she imagined she wanted, Eliza was wretched.

Her sense of outrage equaled society's. Great men had loved her but matrons, even those married to poor men or fools, held her in contempt.

In the third year of her relationship with Stephen, in order to command to respect of those who would not acknowledge her worth, she coerced Stephen into marriage. Typically, she preferred to stage a drama whose outcome was inevitable than to ask a favor. She knew he would marry her if she were dying, and in the arcane pharmacology of prostitutes, was a drug which simulated this approach of death.

It was available in any household. Ergot is the fungus which attacks rye in cold wet weather. The spoiled flour is usually thrown away; but midwives and prostitutes knew that the evil smelling grain could cause violent contractions in the big involuntary muscles: heart, stomach and uterus. For centuries midwives used ergot to induce birth, to abort a fetus, or to stop post partum bleeding. Doctors, knowing its reputation as an abortant, ignored its value; just as midwives, knowing its worth, ignored its dangerous side effects.

In the Middle Ages, the plagues of St. Anthony's Fire, which regularly swept Eastern Europe, were caused by stores of blighted rye. It was called Fire for its pain; Anthony's for the saint's crutch-shaped cross. The swollen, black and purple limbs of its victims were, or would usually be , amputated. But in the fall, with the gathering of a new harvest, St. Anthony's plague always abated; just as yellow fever abated after the first frost.

Midwives, not knowing the strength of any particular supply of ergot, relied roughly on experience and superstition. They usually offered a woman in prolonged labor three grains, in the name of the Father, Son and Holy Ghost. Occasionally the blessing was understood ironically, even blasphemously.

The midwives' purpose was often accomplished. But the violence of the drug-induced contractions always drew blood away from the extremities and surface of the body; leaving the skin cold and white, the pulse feeble and erratic, the breath quick and shallow and the limbs numb or paralyzed.

Acting could not suggest death so poignantly. Eliza availed herself of the drug whose effects she had seen at Mother Ballou's, forcing circumstances to her liking without moral reservations, but with considerable courage.

Returning from Philadelphia, Jumel was greeted by servants who told him his mistress was dying. His doctor was there and had already sent for a priest. Assimilating the scene, Jumel was told of Eliza's conversion by desire. *"She wants to meet her God as a married woman."* Weeping, Jumel asked the priest to join them in marriage. Under the circumstances, a rite full of heart-rendering references of death to come. *"That she who wears this ring may abide in Thy peace... that ye may so live that in the life to come... Until death do ye part."*

Tannic acid is the antidote to the alkaloids of ergot, but Jumel's doctor was not privy to Eliza's secret. She asked for cups of tea. In two days she was up and about; and in three, abroad in her carriage.

Jumel would reproach her later, but in 1804, still blinded by love, he rejoiced at her miraculous recovery. He married her again, formally, in New York's sole Catholic church; poor, unhallowed St. Peters, whose very cornerstone was laid without benefit of clergy and in total ignorance of Catholic ritual.

Stephanus Jumel married Elizabethum Brown for the second time on the nineteenth of April in 1804. Jumel lavished gifts on the church; and when he was in

France again, still grateful for his wife, he sent the proud new cathedral of St. Patrick's on Prince Street, a gold ostensoire, chalice and ciborium for the exposed Host; as well as vestments embroidered in silver and gold for the Holy Seasons of the calendar.

11

"I contemplate you with such a strange mixture of
humility, admiration, reverence, love and pride... that
very little superstition would be necessary to make me
worship you as a superior being; such enthusiasm does
your character excite in me... My vanity would be
greater if I had not been placed near you; and yet my
pride is our relationship. I had rather not live than not
be the daughter of such a man."
Theodosia Burr

That summer, in 1804, as Madame Jumel
gloried in her titles, Burr challenged Hamilton to a duel
and killed him. The cognoscenti assumed they fought
for the honor of a woman, if only because the nature of
Hamilton's offense was, by tacit agreement, even in
private correspondence, never explicit.

Eliza wondered if the stolen letter forced Burr
to defend her. But the letter had been stolen eight
years before; she knew that neither man would fight
for a prostitute's honor.

Nor was the matter political. It was Burr's
habit, part of his rigid personal code, to ignore political
slander and all attacks on his character. Gore Vidal's
intuition seems valid. It seems obvious that Hamilton
called Burr's love for his daughter incestuous. He
flaunted the relationship. No one who knew him
could doubt that he would kill or be killed for
Theodosia.

Her birthday fell on June 23rd, the day the date
of the duel was confirmed; and although she was in
South Carolina with her husband, Burr gave a party in

her honor, setting her portrait at her old place at the table.

On the eve of the duel, he wrote his daughter: *"I am indebted to you, my dearest Theodosia, for a very great portion of the happiness which I have enjoyed in this life. You have completely satisfied all that my heart and affections had hoped or even wishes... all that my ambition and vanity had fondly imagined. Adieu."*

To his son-in-law, he wrote: *"If it be my lot to fall, I commit to you all that is most dear to me, my reputation and my daughter. Let me entreat you to stimulate and aid Theodosia in the stimulation of her mind. It is essential to her happiness and yours... But if you differ with me as the importance of this, suffer me to ask it as a last favor."*

Hamilton, too, spent that evening writing. He tentatively apologized for his attacks on Burr. Although he had challenged James Monroe and been saved from his moment of truth by Burr, he said that dueling was against his religious and moral principles. As he had admonished his son, he said he would withhold the first fire. Thus he was assured that if he killed Burr, he would be called innocent; and if he fell, he would die a martyr.

To prevent the latter he armed himself with a weapon whose secret mechanism gave him a split second advantage. As the challenged man, Hamilton provided both weapons. They were identical; but Burr, not knowing his weapon's secret, could not, if he would, have taken its advantage.

On July eleven, at seven in the morning, the antagonists rowed across the Hudson and met on the dueling ledge; a plateau under the heights of the Palisades, six feet wide, eleven paces long, twenty feet above the river. They saluted each other formally, and at the given word, fired simultaneously. Hamilton fell and Burr's movement toward him was restrained by his seconds.

At nine a bulletin was posted on the Tontine door: **General Hamilton has been mortally wounded by Aaron Burr.** Jumel and his fellows hung on the hourly bulletins; and as the shocking story was told and retold, Burr's role was made to seem villainous.

With iron poise, he had gone from Weehawken to Richmond Hill to meet his nephew for breakfast. Hours after, when the young man heard the terrible news, he was incredulous. *"It is quite impossible,"* he said. *"I have just had breakfast with Colonel Burr and he made no mention of it."*

Again Burr wrote to Theodosia: *"I have been shivering all day and although in perfect health. I have just now at sunset had a fire in my library and am sitting near it enjoying it - if that word may be applicable to anything done in solitude... I must drop the subject, lest it lead me to another on which I have imposed silence on myself."*

Hamilton died at two the next afternoon, leaving his widow with six children and debts amounting to $55,000.

The Tontine merchants resolved to close their shops, to lower their flags and to wear mourning for thirty days. The life of the city stopped altogether for Hamilton's funeral. The forlorn salute of the Battery's thirteen cannon was answered by an English frigate and two French men-of-war. Forty towns took the name Hamilton. The public's surging sense of outrage demanded a victim; and a coroner's jury met to satisfy that need. Again, the news was nailed to the Tontine door.

"Aaron Burr, esquire, Vice President of the United States, not having the fear of God before his eyes, but being moved and seduced by the Devil...with force of arms...feloniously and of his malice of aforethought, did make an assault...with a certain pistol of the value of one dollar, charged and loaded with gun powder and a leaden bullet...held in his right hand to, at, and against the right side of the belly of the said Alexander Hamilton."

In spite of the fact that almost every prominent man in New York had been involved in a duel, Burr was indicted for murder.

Ignoring the judgments of New York and New Jersey juries, he continued to preside over the Senate as Vice President of the United States. On New Year's Eve, when he took leave of that office, his colleagues wept, and the Senate moved to thank him for 'the dignity, impartiality and ability' with which he discharged his duties. Thus, still buoyant, Burr left public office forever; and barred from politics or the practice of law, he turned to the West and the territories that belonged to Spain.

In 1807, he was arrested for treason. Long before a verdict could be reached, President Jefferson called him guilty; and Americans drank: *"To Aaron Burr: May his treachery to his country exalt him to the scaffold, and may hemp be his escort to the Republic of dust and ashes."* Burr maintained his customary calm.

He was found innocent but held guilty in the public mind. John Jacob Astor financed his flight from America, giving him $25,000 for Richmond Hill, its furnishings and the huge tract of land which is known as Greenwich Village. Astor, according to his golden

70

rule, *'Buy acres, sell lots,'* disposed of Richmond Hill, and Burr's stately home became a squalid tavern.

12

"O what a potent power is motherhood! All women
alike fight fiercely for a child."
Euripides

Ironically, the frustration which was to torment
and baffle Madame Jumel as long as she lived, began
with her marriage and her longing to be accepted by
persons of quality. She endlessly counted her carnal
conquests of great men. There was no social reward in
it, nor did her honorable title appease the merciless
matrons of New York. A camel could pass through
the eye of a needle as easily as a whore into society.
Then, perversely, Eliza missed the familial comfort of
Freelove's home and thought well of Providence. Like
Madame, her sister Lavinia had borne an illegitimate
child. Again it was delivered by Freelove Ballou. But
Lavinia, raised in the sturdy virtue of the Ballou
household, kept her baby. The following year, when
she moved to New York, it was not to seek her
fortune, but to marry the father of her child, a man
named Jones.

Lavinia named her daughter Ann Eliza,
obviously to renew old affections and the bond of
blood. Seeing the infant, Madame felt a quickening of
maternity, and yearned for the baby she had
abandoned, Little George Washington.

It is a measure of Madame's boldness, as well as
her loneliness, that every day she drove to Lavinia's
tenement and parked her conspicuous carriage in front
of the door. At least once Stephen went with her; and

while Madame played with Ann Eliza, Stephen listened to Mr. Jones play the fiddle.

From Lavinia, Madame learned that their sister Polly was dead. The annals do not record her death. At the time of the trial for Madame's estate, only Daniel Hull still remembered, or cared, that Polly had ever lived. *"She died in North Providence, somewhere up at what they called the Woods, at the house of a doctoress called Missus Angel."* Mr. Angel made the coffin, Hull's father rode out to identify the body.

Reuben Ballou was dead too. Freelove lived in the old house with her son William, and devoted herself to little George. *"He's such a pretty boy,"* Lavinia told Madame.

Recklessness had become her matter of course. When Madame involved Stephen with Lavinia, she jeopardized her marriage, for Lavinia knew her as a whore and the mother of a bastard. Now she determined to claim her son and deceive her husband, to tell Stephen that George was the child of her dead sister, Polly Bowen.

She planned to seduce Mother Ballou. Lavinia brought the old woman to New York on a packet ship. Madame invited them to her Mansion. They arrived at nine; Stephen dined with them at two. Nothing was said about the business at hand, nor could they speak in front of Jumel. They ate in majestic leisure. A prosperous household, they served roast beef surrounded by potatoes, presented with bowls of broth; a course of peas and baked eggs followed by baked fish and raw cabbage. Entrees were followed by pastry sweets, fruit, cheese and pudding. Madeira was served with everything.

The ladies excused themselves then, leaving

73

Stephen to drink as much as he pleased.

Then Madame, sure that her married status, her Mansion and lavish table had overwhelmed her aunt, spoke up. She wanted her baby back. She could provide for George better than Freelove could. She could make him a gentleman. Jumel was willing to send him to college and after that to France.

Freelove would not argue. *"You gave him to me, Betsy, and I'm going to keep him."* The child was Widow Ballou's reason for living.

"But Auntie he's my baby and I need him," Freelove was not moved. Madame called her *"ugly and hard hearted."*

Lavinia sided with Freelove. *"Best leave him in Providence, Betsy."*

A round of envy added to the tension. Lavinia was raised in a functional home. Madame's sins had been rewarded, and Freelove's virtue overwhelmed them both. Freelove had raised her own son, one of Phebe's and, for the past eight years, she had raised Eliza's. Lavinia and the old woman called Madame *"biggity"*. That they should feel superior appalled her. Madame's self-love, always dependent on the mirror-image that others reflected, was deeply hurt.

Neither Lavinia nor Freelove would live long enough to describe the scene in court. But Ann Eliza would repeat what she had been told of family tradition, of *"the high words and great dispute,"* She did not say that blackmail was implicit. But obviously Freelove could, if she chose, tell Stephen that Madame was the mother of a bastard.

Madame took to bed with a headache. When Freelove was back in Providence, Madame tried again to enlist Lavinia's help. *"I could do as much for Ann*

Eliza as I could for George," Madame said. Lavinia could not be bribed and the sisters quarreled so bitterly, that visiting between them stopped altogether.

Yellow fever broke out in New York. As usual the malignancy began between the Fly Market and the Old Dock. It spread west from the Burlington Slip as far as Pearl Street, then like brush fire in every direction. One third of the city was evacuated as rich men and their families retreated to Harlem or Brooklyn or New Ark across the Hudson. Except for howling dogs and hammering coffin makers, the waterfront was silent.

In 1807 the waterfront was deserted again, not because of yellow fever, but because of Jefferson's Embargo. To merchants like Jumel, the Embargo was the greater malignancy. American merchant ships were forbidden to enter foreign ports. Even coastal trade was restricted; and the owner of a vessel traveling north or south had to post bond for twice the value of the cargo. The quays were deserted; the great ships dismantled - their decks cleared, their hatches battened. Boxes, bales, barrels and casks no longer filled the narrow streets. Grass grew in the slips. Scores of counting houses were for let, and in the course of five months, one hundred and twenty-five merchants declared bankruptcy.

The whole country suffered. Jefferson had rather America withdraw from the seas than be drawn into the bloodbath of the Napoleonic Wars. Britain's Order of Council declared any American vessel which did not first sail to England for a license, was fair game for their warships. Even vessels bound for the Indies were included in the Orders. While on the Continent, in any port controlled by the French, American ships were seized at will. Sometimes Napoleon claimed that he claimed American ships to help Jefferson enforce his embargo; sometimes he claimed American vessels were English ships in disguise. In either case he confiscated them.

Even in these circumstances the firm of Jumel and Desorby prospered. Their ships continued to sail from Spanish Florida to the Indies and from Nova Scotia to Europe - but not without harassment. Of their ships, a brig was driven into Halifax by the British Cambria. The Margaret Tuigey was held up by the British Nemesis, the Stephen was detained in Bermuda, The Minerva was lost in a tremendous sea; and the Prosper and Purse were forced into the harbor of Bayonne, where they were confiscated by Napoleon. Jumel kept his accounts in a parchment duodecimal, listing debits and credits in his cramped, almost, illegible hand. The sums were satisfactory.

Twice in his absence, Madame Jumel went back to Providence. The first time she escorted the body of her old protector, Captain Mason, and stayed at the home of his widow. As friends and relatives called on the bereaved woman, Madame saw old friends and acquaintances. Daniel Hull paid his respects.

"I heard the women talking about the dead man." Hull told the court. *"And I saw her, Madame Jumel, at Captain Mason's house. She said she came to see about her boy."*

Madame told everyone in Providence, except Freelove that she came to claim little George. Still she dreaded a confrontation with her twelve-year-old son as much as the anger of the Aunt.

Another witness, Maria Hall, told the court that she was a child when her mother brought her to call on

76

Widow Mason. *"I was playing with the kittens and didn't really notice until Madame Jumel (my mother said it was very wicked to call her Bowen or Betsy) said she came to see her little boy. Then I inquired where he was and they said he boarded with Missus Ballou uptown. I asked if they was going to fetch him so I could play with him, and they said he was a deal too big; and my mother said, 'Madame, he's such a pretty boy'."*

Madame could handle danger with better grace than frustration. She never confronted Freelove again, but she found a surrogate. When she returned to New York, she had a child with her; not George Washington, but kin, an orphan, a six year old named Mary Browns or Bowens or Bones. Perhaps she was the child of her dead sister Polly. (Madame, of course had two sisters named Polly; Polly Bowen and Polly Clarke).

Jumel accepted Mary and she remained their only child. Perhaps Madame would not subject herself to another pregnancy; perhaps she was unable to conceive, or Stephen unable to beget. Whether they legally adopted Mary or not, they called her Mary Eliza Jumel and withheld no part of their affection.

Madame soon went back to Providence not to claim her son, but to extract from the people who knew her the homage she felt was her due. This time she reserved Washington's room at the Golden Ball, a large room to the right of the balcony where the President stood to review the veterans of the Continental Army. She let it be known that on a certain evening, she would stand on that balcony to lecture the provincials of Providence on etiquette in the court of France. She had forgotten how many in the audience would be veterans of her bed.

77

Old Hull remembered. *"It was evening,"* he said. *"I was coming down Main Street with a parcel of my comrade boys and there was a crowd, maybe more than a hundred boys and men around the tavern the Frenchmen kept on Benefit Street. Betsy came out on the platform; it was covered up piazza-like, and she said she was Madame Jumel and had been admitted to the court of France. And they began to hoot so I couldn't hear what she said. You know how a mob is, hissing and hooting and hollering and one thing and another. Then they began to shout, BETSY BOWEN! BETSY BOWEN! BETSY BOWEN! and she went back in."*

She would often be paid in that coin; humiliation for hubris, ridicule for grandiosity. She was driven as much by horror of the sordidness she had endured, as by her rage at society's contempt for a prostitute.

She knew society should not judge women more harshly for selling than they judge men for buying. She knew that in the 18th century, the contract of marriage was usually an exchange of sex for security, and it was seldom a fair contract. As Franklin wrote, *"Married women are kept in a state of dependence which defrauds their hearts and insults their intelligence."* No husband of Madame Jumel could make that statement.

It is the function of society to exclude "inferiors,' and society met Madame's advances with consummate cruelty. She protected herself with fantasy. Accepting only occasional corrections from reality, she followed the supreme law of her ego: My worth shall not be diminished.

13

"The surroundings householders crave are glorified,
ghost written autobiographies."
T. N. Tobsjohn-Giddings

Jumel did everything possible to advance his
wife's impossible ambition. In 1810 he bought her the
Morris Mansion on Harlem Heights, where in her
heart, she could bask in the power and glory of the
men who had lived there; including, of course, the man
for whom she had named her son.

She didn't know that the house had had
sentimental value for Washington too. He had courted
his first mistress, the spirited, wealthy Mary Philipse;
who, while Washington fought Indians married his
comrade, Roger Morris. Morris built the house for his
bride, and in their prenuptial agreement, deeded the
mansion in her name.

Years later, when Washington commandeered
the house (Morris was a Tory) he sent a message to his
former sweetheart. *"I beg the favor of having my
compliments presented to Mrs. Morris."* As Burr said, the
Revolution was a civil war.

As President, Washington paid a nostalgic visit
to his old Headquarters bringing with him his
republican court, his cabinet and their wives. Late in
the afternoon they sat down to a stately catered dinner.
Thus in 1810, when the house became hers, Madame
could truthfully say, that every President of the United
States had dined in her dining room. There had been
only three: Washington, Adams and Jefferson.

Madame never knew Burr wanted to exchange

Richmond Hill for the Morris Mansion. His daughter had urged the move. *"In New York it would be a principality. And there is something stylish, respectable and suitable for you to have such a handsome country seat."* Burr said he liked his daughter's reasoning. But he took no initiative and seven months later, he could not. He had killed Hamilton.

For ten thousand dollars, Mt. Morris became the principality of Madame Jumel. Its one hundred and eighty acres stretched from the Harlem to the Hudson River. There were meadows and oak woods, salt marshes for hay, a berth for a boat, mud flats for clamming, an apple orchard, quince trees, three good gardens, a large barn (where, after Washington fled, the British quartered two hundred prisoners), stables and coach house. Two gate houses flanked a huge bowed gate. The isolated Mansion still stands as an oasis in the Spanish and Dominican Harlem.

The house is formal. Like Richmond Hill, the facade has pillars and pediment, balcony and quoined corners simulating stone. There are great halls, foyers really, on the first and second floors; which, with their adjoining rooms, are separated by a narrow passage from octagonal rooms above and below.

Timber for the house was cut in the Morris woods; shaped with broad ax and chisel; secured for the centuries with white oak pins. As insulation against winter cold and summer heat, the walls were lined with English brick. A basement kitchen runs the full length of the house. On the third floor are rooms for slaves. Morris carved the date on the keystone arch of the baronial hall: 1758.

Thus the house was fifty-two years old when Madame took possession. She and Stephen slept in

Washington's bedroom; adopted Mary slept in Hamilton's. On the balcony where Washington and his officers watched the burning of New York, Madame had two fiddlers play operatic arias to wake her in the morning. She called the old Courts Martial room her drawing room. Every evening the little family dined where all the Presidents had dined. With surprising tact, she called the place Mt. Stephen.

The house which had been a common farm as well as an inn was in bad repair. Madame devoted herself to restoration. Since her taste was essentially vulgar, the idea of restoring Mary Morris's decor was a happy one. Madame sent to Paris for reproductions of Mary's veridian panels with their morning glory friezes. She had the octagonal gate houses, the coach house and stables repaired. She laid walks and planned gardens. M. Jumel built a fish pond. Madame enjoyed the long indulgence of bringing the house and its furnishings to a state of perfection.

Her motive was straightforward, to restore the mansion to its former fame as a center of hospitality. Mary Morris had been a famous hostess. The de Peysters, the de Lanceys, the Van Courtlands, Bayards and Livingstons had been frequent guests. Madame sent two hundred invitations engrossed in French to the social elite of the City. The names had not changed. She hired the chef from the City Hotel; and musicians from the Park Theater played in front of her veridian panels.

All of Madame's invitations were acknowledged. The banquet was a triumph. She was giddy with pleasure; until in the course of time, she understood that she had been the object of society's curiosity; and again, of their mockery. No invitation

81

was ever returned.

The mansion's eighteen commodious rooms became a monument to the loneliness of the Jumels: but Madame was obdurate.

Charity was then as it is now an entrance to society. After the death of her husband, Madame's neighbor on the Heights, Mrs. Alexander Hamilton, devoted herself to a refuge for orphans. So did Madame Jumel. St. Peters, where Eliza and Stephen had been married, had become an asylum for French children orphaned by the Napoleonic Wars. Stephen paid the bills. Madame sponsored a school for indigent children run by Ursuline nuns imported from Ireland in the pious hope of making converts. Again, Stephen paid the bills.

Meanwhile, thinking of adopting another child, perhaps one of his own kin, Stephen looked for distant relatives. He found a cousin living in the Province of Quebec. The young man was not adoptable, but in the goodness of his heart, Stephen arranged for his passage to Bordeaux so that he could meet other Jumels and explore his ancestral roots.

"I knew who she was, you see," Catherine Williams told the Court. *"It was at Mrs. McCullers' in Brooklyn; and Mrs. Jumel was very genteelly dressed with a white bonnet and veil. I noticed particularly, because I wanted to see her countenance. It didn't appear to me as how she was very intellectual looking. And she had a frail little girl with her - white, not colored. I looked at her very attentive too; and I asked. 'Is she your daughter?' And she said not - that she was adopted.*

Then I said to her, 'Mrs. Jumel, Mrs. McCullers observed to me that you come from Providence, so will you tell me your unmarried name?' And she said Bowen.

'Bowen? Bowen? Bowen?' I said. 'Are you related to the doctor's family?"

Madame Jumel's poise was not shaken. "My mother was a widow," she said, "and resided there but a short time in Providence. I myself resided there but a short time. My connections are dead and I have no family that you might think of." She asked Catherine Williams to call. "I live in Harlem, Mrs. Williams. The house has a very nice prospect. You might admire it."

Eventually someone from Providence told Stephen that his wife had borne a bastard and they quarreled catastrophically. Henry Nodine, a carpenter hired to work on the Mansion, told the Court what he overheard. Plainly he was in sympathy with his master. He imitated his accent:

"My Eliza, you tell me one big story! You never tell Mr. Jumel you have one little boy in Providence - else Mr. Jumel, he not marry you. You tell Mr. Jumel you very sick and want to die one married woman. Mr. Jumel he marry you, and in two days you ride around in your carriage. You tell Mr. Jumel one big story."

"Then," said Nodine, "that Madame admitted the truth. And the language she used to him in reply! She swore and cursed and cursed and then she threatened to kill him with the pistol she kept and carried."

Madame's pistols came up in court again and again. On every occasion one lawyer or another objected. The objections were always sustained. Some peace, an armed peace, was made between husband and wife.

It was broken, according to the testimony of Ann Eliza Ballou, when Stephen made sexual advances of such a frightening nature toward fourteen-year-old Mary, that on two different occasions, she ran away and hid in the house of her Aunt Lavinia.

Perhaps Stephen saw the deflowering of his adopted daughter as his prerogative, a grand blanc's droit de seigneur. Mary was not his begetting. He may have denied the reality of incest. Probably, most deeply and half consciously, his advances against Mary were vengeance, sexual revenge for Madame's sexual manipulation. Perhaps it was sadder than that. Perhaps his alienation from Eliza was such that Mary was the only loving person in his life, her admiration his only comfort. Turning to her for closeness, he may have found his sudden compulsion truly shameful.

Certainly Madame did. She never forgave him. *"She held it over him,"* Ann Eliza would testify. *"From that time on she was in charge."* Probably at this time Madame absolved herself of prostitution. Her righteousness, grounded in denial of her past, became absolute.

Stephen's joy in life was permanently extinguished. He would never appear again as an open, great-hearted man; rather pathetic, ineffectual and petty.

Mary's hurt was beyond reparation. The experience confirmed her timidity with men, and would ensure her frigidity in marriage. She never escaped from Madame, but remained in a state of dependency.

Though the matter was buried as unspeakable, it continued to work its harm and the hateful ambiance of the Mansion was extraordinary.

Madame decided to abandon it. Flight seemed advisable for several reasons: to leave behind the scene of social humiliation, Stephen's offense, and the people who knew of both. Stephen had reasons of his own.

He had committed some malfeasance against his partner, Benjamin Desorby; the nature of which, was well known to Madame. It was serious enough to put an ocean between them. They had lived in the Mansion five years when they decided to return to France.

France was still the country of Madame's fantasies. No one there could revive her past, except those aspects she doted on and talked about. She was, as always, ripe for adventure.

Before they sailed, on the very day of their departure, in June, 1815, Madame persuaded Stephen *"in consideration of the love and affection he bore her"* to deed the Mansion to her *"for and during her natural life."* At Madame's death the estate would revert to Stephen's heirs. Mary was his only heir. Madame was content. With Mary as both buffer and binder, they embarked on the Eliza and sailed for Royan at the Mount of the Gironde in Les Charentes.

There, by a remarkable coincidence, Madame again met Napoleon, engaged his attention, offered him hope, and received his favors.

14

"Nothing is more difficult, and therefore more precious
than to be able to decide."
Napoleon

France was mutilated, occupied, bankrupt. Few
ventures in history have been more disastrous than
Napoleon's Hundred Days, the lapse between his
escape from Elba and his defeat at Waterloo. Unable to
relinquish power, be clung to its illusion. He outlined
further plans of battle and asked for the powers of a
dictator. *"Tell you brother,"* said the Marquis de
Lafayette to Lucien Bonaparte, *"that if he does not
submit his resignation, we will notify him of his
dethronement."*
Napoleon abdicated for the second time in
spiritual anguish. He left the Elysee Palace and
retreated to Malmaison, where depersonalized with
shock and horror, he waited for France to call him
back. He sent an impatient message to the Chamber of
Deputies: *"Explain...that I have no intention of taking
power again. I will command the Army...defeat the
enemy...crush him. Then I will depart."*
"Is he mocking us?" said Fouché. Such was the
general longing for peace, that when the Czar rode
through the streets of Paris, women who had lost
husbands, sons, brothers, fathers and lovers in Russia
crowded around him to kiss his boots.
As Napoleon permitted himself to understand
what indeed he knew, that France had repudiated him,
he began to dream of a new life in the New World. *"I
might plow the earth, live off the produce of the fields, end*

where man began." He asked for every book written on the United States.

His family joined him: His mother; his sisters Caroline and Hortense; his brothers, Joseph, Lucien and Jerome. The Countess Walewska came with Napoleon's little son. He sent them away. Nothing roused him from his apathy. Hortense forced her way into his study. *"The French are not worthy of you, since they've forsaken you. If it is to be America, get to a port before the English discover your intent."* Joseph left for England to buy forged passports, and Napoleon asked the banker La Fitte to find him a ship.

"Eh Bien, M. La Fitte," said Napoleon, *"The United States is a boring country to live in. So, it's goodbye to all the charming conversations and cultivated society of Paris. Farewell to the arts. Farewell to science. Except for a common hatred of England, I shall have no sympathy with the Americans."*

La Fitte had the frigates Medusa and La Salle prepared for the voyage to America and moved to the port of Rocheforte above Royan. Those who loved the Emperor came to bid him farewell. He talked only of the future when they would meet in America. *"I will send for your boy,"* he promised Caroline; but he lingered. The delay frightened Joseph. *"The essential thing is to get to America."* Hortense gave him a belt into which she had sewn a diamond necklace. He said goodbye to his mother and stood weeping in Josephine's room. At last, after fifteen days, he left for Rochefort in a yellow calash without armorial bearings - followed nevertheless by an impressive suite of officers and servants.

But France, in collusion with England, had prepared a mousetrap. The British ships Bellerphron,

Myidian, Phoebe, the Superb and the Arachon blockaded the port of Rochefort, the mouth of the Gironde at Royan and the estuary of La Teste. Any French ship bound for America would have to run a British blockade

The captains of La Salle and the Medusa were wholly devoted to the Emperor. *"Sire, we will let ourselves be sunk rather than cease fire before Your Majesty gives the order."* But Napoleon did not wish to die running from the British; and since England could not legally search the ship of a neutral country, he imagined he could escape on an American vessel. He sent a messenger to the Prefect of the Port, *"What are the chances? Could use be made of an American vessel?"*

He was advised to go in a small rowboat as far as the Seudre, from the Seudre to Royan on horseback. From Royan, two vessels, the Bayadere and the Infatigable, would carry him and his entourage to the United States. Meanwhile a corvette was made ready, so that at any moment, if the estuary were left unguarded, he could escape.

Still he waited; for tides, for Joseph, for France to ask him to return. Two American privateers said they would sacrifice themselves running the blockade: *"But let the Emperor hasten."*

Joseph came bearing passports with English names - with an English doctor and an American interpreter.

At this time, after a voyage of thirty-eight days, the Eliza reached the mouth of the Gironde and the Jumels - surely Stephen had little choice - were embroiled in the Emperor's intrigues. Through General Bertrand or Joseph or perhaps another of Napoleon's emissaries, Jumel offered the Eliza as a

88

means of escape. The Emperor could hide in an empty wine keg. Napoleon was appalled at the indignity. Madame, to whom Mt. Stephen now belonged, offered her Mansion as a place of refuge. The Emperor was grateful. He did not commit himself.

He decided to board La Salle. He said he would leave his yellow calash to the Prefect of the Port; but the Admiral refused to accept such a dangerous gift.

A soldier came to carry Napoleon on his back to the long boat of La Salle. Men lining the shore shouted, *"Long live the Emperor!"* *"Farewell, my friends,"* Napoleon murmured.

As he boarded La Salle, the mousetrap closed. He would have no further communication with the mainland. Orders had been given that if he ever set foot in France again, he would be arrested for high treason. Furthermore, the captain of the Bellerphone had orders to search all vessels, French or otherwise; and to use all means to intercept the fugitive *"upon whose capture the repose of Europe depends."* La Salle took the Emperor to an island in the harbor of Aix, where a tiny villa served as a palace. An iron balcony opened on the sea. It was very hot. Napoleon slept.

Rousing himself, he asked Baudin if he could still arrange an escape on one of the vessels in the mouth of the Gironde. *"I can do it less easily than the week before,"* said Baudin. *"I have got rid of the means on which I had counted. But let the Emperor come with a bag and a valet and one or two friends of sense and courage tomorrow night without noise..."* Napoleon would not. Could not.

Six young officers proposed an alternative to General Bertrand. Napoleon should purchase two luggers, which thanks to their shallow draft, could hug the coast. These would take the Emperor to St. Martin de Re, where a smack was ready for sea. Napoleon ordered the luggers bought and equipped. Joseph arrived saying, *"Hurry, Let the Emperor take the vessel waiting in the mouth of the Gironde, the Eliza,"* The Emperor was depressed. Joseph asked if he might surrender in his brother's place, try to deceive the British until he was on the high seas. Napoleon would not accept such a sacrifice. Other plots were suggested and not acted upon. Napoleon waited in confusion, uncertainty and dread. Baudin approached Jumel. What they said is not known, nor does it matter.

The tragedy moved in stately measure. Napoleon decided to escape in the luggers. His luggage was taken aboard, while a long boat rowed to the Bellerphron with a flag of truce to mask the Emperor's escape. At midnight, the six young officers who had volunteered to man the luggers were arrested.

Napoleon gave up all hope of reaching America. Still deceiving himself, he decided to surrender to the British on the Bellerphron. Wearing the green uniform of the Light Horse of the Imperial Guard, the Grand Cross of the Legion of Honor, and the Order of the Iron Crown, he embarked on a brig which carried him to the British vessel. *"The fortunes of war have brought me to my cruelest enemy."* He murmured. *"I trust in his fairness."* He said he would like to live in a country house ten or twelve leagues from London. But Napoleon was not a prisoner of England. He was a captive of the Coalition of Kings. They decided his disposition, his exile to that volcanic rock in the South Atlantic called St. Helena.

Sometime the next day, the day after Napoleon's surrender, General Bertrand delivered the

Emperor's yellow calash to Monsieur and Madame Jumel. In it, either by design or mistake, was the chest which Napoleon had carried from Moscow. Madame would say it was full of treasures given in return for services rendered.

15

"O Mother, the King spoke to me."
"And what did he say, darling?"
"Get out of my way, you bastard."
Irish

The Emperor's yellow calash had no armorial bearings. But Madame, as if she were herself a principality, appropriated the eagle; and to distinguish her emblem from that of Napoleon's late army and those of Prussia, Russia and the United States - as well as those of the Byzantine and Holy Roman Empires (whose names she had never heard), she substituted a quiver of arrows for the body of the Bird. With this devise emblazoned on the panels of her carriage, and on the door of her house in the Rue de Rivoli, she drew immediate attention to herself. Her eagle and Bonaparte's carriage were powerful charms. The story she told of Napoleon's last hours in France was deeply moving, at least to the distraught Bonaparte nobility, who embraced the rich merchant and his beautiful American wife.

Mary was put in a school for foreign Catholic girls. Probably in her mind, she saw herself as abandoned, left among strangers in a strange country, as a kind of punishment. Stephen could hardly protest that Mary felt forsaken, and Madame did not really want to be burdened by the wretched adolescent. Stephen answered her pitiful letters with conventional fondness. Madame never made the effort.

A courtesan's gifts are organized under ego. Madame had never given herself wholly to love. Her interest always lay in her power to captivate. Such women grow cold in middle age. It is not likely that she replaced her exhausted husband with a lover.

The new regime blessed the coldness of women. With the restoration of the new Bourbon monarch, Louis XVII, ladies suddenly became too delicate and dignified for carnal pleasure. As if sex were an animal to be caged, women confined their bodies, bound their breasts with steel husks, hid their throats in stiff ruffs, compressed their waists, concealed their arms in pagoda or leg o'mutton sleeves; and as if they were not crotched creatures, they unified themselves below the waist with petticoat stiffened, bell-like skirts. Thus fortified they played their roles as guardians of morality. Madame founded herself in that society in the same sense, and as surely, as Burr founded the Bank of Manhattan. The Age coincided with her inclination, her new righteousness. She turned avidly to French society.

The names of the titled persons with whom she exchanged invitations, acknowledgments and regrets are preserved. No letter from a member of nobility was too trivial to be thrown away.

Thus Madame could always prove that she counted among her friends, the Duchess de Berry, the Duke and Duchess d'Alzac, the Duchess de Charot; and although the basis for intimacy is obscure, the Countess Marcelle Tasher de la Pagerie, whose husband was an uncle of the Empress Josephine, made her home with the Jumels, or rather with Madame. Stephen traveled most of the time.

The resident countess had access to relics of Napoleon's grandeur. Although the Bourbon restoration made such memorabilia embarrassing to most Frenchmen, Madame coveted them as evidence of her intimacy with Napoleon. Thus she acquired the bed where he slept as First Counsul; the slipper chairs of Hortense, Queen of Holland; eight dining room chairs covered with green silk and gold stars, the tapestry where the Emperor rested his feet when he played chess at Malmaison, a tea service decorated with acanthus leaves and Bonaparte bees, a tortoise and ebony box painted by Josephine, the gold and enamel watch the Empress wore at her coronation; and a gold and cloisonne clock belonging to the Emperor on which Madame had engraved, to Madame Jumel, Napoleon, 1815, linking her name with his as if the clock had been a gift. Indeed, it had been found in the war chest in the back of the yellow calash. Dearest, and of the greatest intrinsic value, were diamonds which had belonged to Josephine: Her tiara, necklace, bracelets and ear rings; treasures of whose pedigree Madame, at least, was assured.

She had become in a real sense, her own creation, a work of art. Her gowns, her diamonds, her carriage, her Bonaparte accessories were essential props. She lived for the eye of the beholder. She was forty, almost in the prime of her beauty.

With perfect tact, she made her home and carriage available not only to the Countess de la Pagerie, but to her friends. Letters like this attest her generosity. *"My dear Madame Jumel, it is for tomorrow that mama has an appointment with M. Roy, the Minister of Finance. Would you kindly let her have the carriage which she wouldn't keep long, if that would not inconvenience you. She would be greatly obliged if you would send it tomorrow evening at eleven o'clock..."*

Because of the Countess, Madame had access at

Court. But the reality fell short of her pent-up expectations. When she had seen herself as the Princess Capet, she had not imagined royal tolerance. She was presented to Louis XVIII. He smiled and murmured something about her yellow carriage. She longed for more.

Her provincial merchant husband was not a social asset. But had he, in fact, had the grace of a prince, it would have made no difference. He had no time to play the role. At the threshold of old age, he bore the increasing burden of Madame's demands; forced to channel his waning energies into new, speculative enterprises. He traveled, recklessly risking his capitol, buying French goods to sell in America through his agent there, M. Durand. Madame's ambition was insupportable - like a millstone thrown to a drowning man.

He passed what men called The Grand Climacteric, his sixtieth birthday. The Climacteric had sickened Washington, who found that milestone in route to his death infinitely depressing. Jumel, burdened as he was by a demanding wife, loss of self-respect, and sudden financial jeopardy, had not found it less traumatic.

Madame determined to make him a courtier. With the hubris that made her dangerous, she composed a letter for the King. The document is unsigned, undated, still waiting, as it were, to be copies, embossed and embellished with ribbons. *"Sire,"* she dictated (the letter is not in her own hand). *"Every time I have the honor of seeing Your Majesty, the graciousness with which you have deigned to notice my carriage and the great kindness with which you bow to me, make me feel like writing to you. But once out of Your presence, courage fails me. The return of Your Majesty on_____ "* (the King moved from palace to palace and Madame prudently left the date open) *"I have so ardently wished for, caused me so much joy that I seem to be inspired with new courage to present a petition in favor of my husband.*

My husband left France at the beginning of the Revolution and established a home in New York, U.S.A., with the resolve of never again seeing his native land until the return of the Bourbons. He became a merchant and has been very fortunate in his business. He is so patriotic that he has been unwilling to have commercial relations anywhere except with France. He was the first to introduce la Soiree at wholesale in the United States, and in doing this he has created a demand for French merchandise, bringing in an enormous trade, so that the most celebrated manufacturers of France have worked for him and have sent millions through his business.

He has had the misfortune to lose two of his ships, all loaded and seized by Napoleon and held at the port of Bayonne for which he has never been reimbursed.

His kindness of heart and his directness in business have made him known and loved throughout the United States. He has frequently been offered very honorable and lucrative positions which he has always refused saying he still hoped to see his own country. What a joyous day for him when he got news of the return of the Bourbons! Immediately he made haste to sell his ships and to leave his temporary home which was for him a sort of exile, since it was so far from his dear country.

We came to Paris and he, seeing a great deal of misfortune, was moved by his kindness of heart to set up several manufacturers who are today prosperous. At the same time, he himself has suffered nothing but losses. His lofty nature will not allow him to ask for a place at Court himself, as he thinks he has not yet done enough for his country to deserve such a favor.

But accustomed to being received as persons of high position, and our fortune admitting of our living in excellent style, and having also had the good fortune since our stay in Paris of knowing many ladies of the Court, I often find myself embarrassed. When I see I have no title and my husband no Cross, in spite of all he has done for his country and his devotion to his King, I feel utterly discouraged and beg him to go back to his adopted country. But knowing Your Majesty's extreme kindness, I am inspired with hope that you will no longer ignore a subject so worthy as Stephen Jumel. Whatever post Your Majesty might deign to offer, even without remuneration, it would be the greatest delight to fill, and Your Majesty would find in Stephen Jumel a faithful subject and in his wife, eternal gratitude. "

If she was not ashamed to argue wealth and poverty together, or to call attention to her yellow calash, Stephen was. He reminded her that their Bourbon loyalty would not bear investigation, and that if the story of her infamous carriage were made public, the small favor she enjoyed at the Court of Louis XVIII would be withdrawn.

She was outraged. To reprove him, to prove that his ideas were beneath contempt, she flaunted her association with Napoleon even more recklessly. She had the eagle of the Emperor's army mounted on the roof of her carriage and decked with laurel leaves, as if the Hundred Days had ended in triumph rather than the restoration of the Bourbons. Riding out, exhibiting herself, and expecting acclaim, she attracted an angry mob who would not let her pass. Such an assault on public peace and the King's dignity could not be ignored. The gendarmes who rescued her, arrested her. Jumel paid her bail.

Public shame was unendurable. Madame left France precipitously. She said goodbye to no one, not even to Mary, forcing Stephen to excuse her, to say that she was ill. Perhaps she was. Outrage and frustration could make her sick with awful headaches. Jumel went with her to Bordeaux, and she sailed on the brig Eliza, alone but not without her Bonaparte treasures. Her adventure with nobility had lasted seventeen months.

Madame's bitterness, Jumel's concern and Mary's distress was great. In December, when her mother was in fact at sea, Mary wrote a pathetic letter inviting Eliza to a school function.

"My dear Mama, as the feast of Mlle. Laurau will take place on Thursday next....the Mistress told me to ask you to come; but I told her you would not because you do not like evening rides...But as Wednesday will be a Recreation Day, it would give me great pleasure if you could come and see me and bring my gauze frock and my shoes and gloves and my lace van dyke of muslin...Give my love to dear papa and tell him not to forget his promise in sending for me. And that I wait with impatience for that day, for it is so dreary in this place that the three English young ladies are always crying and at last have run away from school...As it will be very cold when we stay upstairs changing our dresses, if you would ask Mlle. Laurau to let us have a fire in my room. Two or three young ladies have permission to have a fire...My dear mama, I embrace you with a thousand kisses. Believe me to be your fond and dutiful daughter. Mary Eliza Jumel. "

Madame answered six months later from her refuge on the Heights, Mt. Stephen.

16

"Commerce fills the purse but clogs the brain. Beyond
their counting houses, these men have not a single
idea."
Betsy Patterson Bonaparte

As a woman waiting for the birth of her child
will move heavy furniture without knowing what
impels her, so Madame moved to end her life with
Stephen. She worked to secure her estate as an
independent manor; and because, even unconsciously,
she faced life without a husband, she took steps to bind
Mary to her as a dependent and therefore amenable
companion.

The evidence for this lies not in Madame's
letters during this period of separation, but between the
lines in the wretched letters Stephen wrote his wife.
He wrote fluently in a slanting, minuscule hand; and
most often about money. When he wrote about his
business ventures, his words and their characters run
together with an urgency which makes them almost
impossible to decipher. Words tumble out without
order. Tenses fail and the bastard French of Santo
Domingo merges with his awkward English. To
confuse matters further, he described his transactions in
terms of gourdes, the currency of the Indies. What
affection he expressed was perfunctory; and since his
emotions were seldom engaged, legible.

Although most of her letters from this time are
missing, it is obvious that Madame tormented him.
She went for months without writing; then dictated
(probably in front of his associates) affectionate,
infinitely unsatisfactory letters which ignored or

evaded his questions. She dictated in French but signed in English; always writing her formal expression of loyalty *"Your ever faithful, loving wife, Eliza,"* in bold, flowing characters.

"My bonne femme," Stephen wrote, assuming she had arrived safely in New York, *"I hope my prayers concerning your health have been answered. We are at a great distance from one another. The weather has been terrible. I pray to God your crossing was better fated. Day before yesterday, I went to see poor Mary. She started to cry as soon as she saw me. And me too. In spite of your homesickness, what you have left behind! If I care enough to restore your health, you should of us. Everyone hopes to see you again in a year. They haven't heard from you since your return to New York. Me neither, by the way. I enclose some letters I ask you to deliver.*

Nothing has been done in the garden since_____" His writing becomes chaotic, as if he were distraught at the thought of Mt. Stephen. *"Weeds join____, Best keep an eye on____."*

In an ever more troubled hand he wrote about vanities, mirrors and debts. He said he owed 18,000 gourdes. *"I have bought so much for you I cannot buy more unless I receive money. Spend as little as you can. You must economize."*

He wrote again the following week. Obviously he relied on her understanding of his business and her willingness to act as his agent, on his behalf. She ignored him.

Toward the end of May, she wrote for the first time to her unhappy daughter; in English, in her own hand.

"My dear Mary: You have heard of my arrival before this as I wrote your papa...But the vessel departed so

100

soon I had no time to write you; and as you know, I am not fond of writing which will be another excuse. But believe me, my dear Mary, my thought is always of you although I do not write often. My health has been restored to me which is a great consolation as I know ti will be to you. Do not forget, my dear Mary, the sacrifice I made was for your good, which I hope you will profit by - in one year to finish your education and to return to your mama who loves your dearly.

I am engaged at this time in setting your room in order. It is admired by everyone that sees it. Your curtains are of blue satin trimmed with silver fringe and your toilette is the same. Although at this distance, my thought is of you. I remain your affectionate mama, Eliza Jumel."

Adopting mothers sometimes emphasize the sacrifice involved in maternity. Madame, masking her will to rule, would demand a lifetime of gratitude from Mary. As there is carelessness in the repetition, *"my thought is of you,"* so is there callousness in the suggestion that Mary join her at Mt. Stephen. Stephen lived in the expectation that Madame would return to France, that within the year they would be united as a family there.

Mary's was not the only room Madame "set in order." She had the dining room repapered in lily green with a five inch border of gold at the top; and she had the two front rooms paneled. Transforming the Mansion from Colonial English to Empire French required a great deal more.

Meanwhile Stephen continued to write his sorry letters about vanities and mirrors. Part of his shipments were for Madame's use and part she had agreed to sell for his benefit. She had the panels under the dado in the octagonal room filled with mirrors, so that swirling skirts, petticoats and ankles might be reflected. A ballroom for balls she would never give.

Stephen was still preoccupied with mirrors and money. *"...I sent you end of April shipment. I couldn't include that mirror because it hadn't dried yet, but you will receive another set of chairs made by the man in the Rue d'Antonine, the one who worked in plate glass. Don't sell anything until you know the price. You can consult M. Durand, but before you sell anything you must ask me. You must be patient. I need money. I've made big buys and owe 4,000 gourdes, which is 200,000 francs. Don't count on receiving as much as last time. I don't want to buy too much. Think of what you have spent since you left me in France! Although for myself, I don't need 3,000 gourdes a year. Think! Since you left, no carriage. But that is better for me. Keep your health. I cannot repeat it enough. God bless you. Adieu."*

As Stephen slowly and painfully came to understand that Madame was using his shipments, and the moneys from their sale, to refurbish the Mansion; and that she did not intend to join him in France, he was distraught. Then hurt and anger made his letters as difficult to read as if he wrote about matters of business.

"If it had been my intention to run away to France, it was that you would stay with me. I have done everything in my power to make you happy. Certainly if a wife loves her husband, she should live where he is. I had hoped to finish my life in France if I could. This is for life, that you stay with me."

She wasn't ready to surrender the advantages of marriage. She reassured him, and the warmth of her letter persuaded him to make the Atlantic crossing he found so dreadful. She had calculated carefully. Mary's year with Mlle. Laurau was over. Stephen's voyage could coincide with his daughter's homecoming. The thought of reunion resurrected, however fleetingly, the old Stephen, the ardent lover.

"My Lisa," he wrote. "My desire is so great that I cannot ignore it. You will guess what motivates me, my beloved. I am ill with homesickness. That is not a mortal illness, but what suffering! Everyone makes fun of me, not being able to eat. I better be careful to maintain my strength before returning to the States. I will finish. My God, how I miss you."

The reunion was not satisfactory. Stephen spoke of money, and, as her servants would testify, Madame screamed and cursed. Like Mother Ballou in the Providence gaol, she was heard from far away. Stephen was forced to leave Mary with her mother. From the peace of Paris, he wrote bitterly; telling Madame what he had not dared to say to her face.

"I see you planted a lot of fruit trees. I don't know why you do - We didn't do it before our departure. I see you have many guests, yet you say you do not spend much. I think differently. I just want you to spend half of our income. Figure in the income of the house...You will say it is nothing but you have always wanted land.

And to think that you and Mary have nothing to wear! And that Mary has to wear old shoes! Well, I will send for you____and____. And for Mary ____. I will take care of all you ask. But as to mirrors, I have had bad luck. It is too expensive. I do not want to spend so much. I must tell you, your way of doing things! For Heaven's sake, THINK! You think it nothing to cultivate the soil on the road to the stables. I had it done last year. It's no use telling you over and over it's pasture land and *must be left alone for ten years or more. So do what you want. But the more you have done, the more you spend. But do what you want. "*

"*But do what you want,*" became the counterpoint of his counsel. She did, as Stephen said, she loved land with a peasants devotion. But she was learning to think of it as an investment. The medium in which great fortunes were made. Astor and Beekman were rich beyond counting. She studied their progress.

Stephen's letters became pitiful. "*I am always alone and overworked. I spend all my time at the factories. Tomorrow I go to Nimes, with a small detour to Languedoc. From there to Bordeaux. My intention was to take the baths, but the orders of M. Durand have made me go to work again. More than ever I need _____.*

I see you are asking for something. You have need of funds. I hope you have received some by now, since they were sent a long time ago. I see you have several helpers this winter. One needs workers in April, no? I hear from M. Desorby and M. Durand that you spend everything different than what you say. You know well you should do what he tells you. You have to be more careful with your expenses. That is how it is. There is more to say, but I haven't the courage. As for the harvest, one must wait and not sell hay before it is ready. Horses like old hay better..."

Although Madame spent money prodigally, planting orchards and vineyards and extending her holdings, her neighbors on the Heights did not regard her solitary state with sympathy. In spite of Stephen's imagining the house filled with guests, she was as lonely as ever. She tried to restore her relationship with Lavinia Ballou, the half-sister with whom she had quarreled, who had been witness to

104

Stephen's depravity.

Lavinia's husband was dead and she lived with her daughter Ann Eliza on Christopher Street. As she had before, when Stephen was away, when her social ambitions were thwarted and she despaired of making friends, Madame wanted news of her son.

Stephen could not stop her now, nor Freelove, who died while Madame was in France. But George Washington Bowen was twenty-four; not only too old to adopt, but possibly too old to forgive his mother's desertion. Madame would never know. Fearless as she was in other ways, she was afraid to go to Providence to ask him.

Lavinia knew George Washington well. Ann Eliza was seven when Madame visited her home on Christopher Street. When the court questioned her, her answers were surly and terse. *"Yes, I saw Madame at my mother's bakery. I saw her three or four times or maybe four or five. I was playing on the stoop and she didn't get out of her carriage. She didn't do anything I know of. Why, of course, she talked. Sometimes Mother called her Betsy Bowen and sometimes Betsy Jumel. They behaved as if they was very well acquainted, I should think. Well, yes, I expect it was a row of houses, or else it wouldn't be a city; I don't recollect if there was vacant lots. Yes, a street went past the door. Yes, I slept in the house. They didn't turn me outdoors. Yes, I know about her son. George Washington Bowen,"* And for the benefit of the courts she added, *"He is an illegitimate child and he cannot recover the inheritance any more than the farthest stranger in the world."*

Madame would not let go. She arranged to meet Lavinia and Ann Eliza, in a neutral place, somewhere between their homes, on the Blooming

Dale Road. They met half way, but the Ballou women walked, waited in their calico dresses beside the road. Madame, with her plumes and rouches and flounces and lace, drove up in her yellow calash.

"We went on purpose to see her," said Ann Eliza. *"We went walking, but we didn't talk but a few minutes. She kept asking my mother when we could come and see her and mother said, 'We'd rather stay away. We was poor but we was proud. And we didn't care to visit her'."*

So the middle-aged sisters who had walked the streets together, found they had no bond. In her unhappiness, Madame turned again to Stephen, telling him she wanted to return to France.

He answered coldly: *"In your last letter you told me of your desire to come to France. I wish that too. But then you must ask yourself if you intend to return to France, do you mean to make an end to my business dealings? Will you sell all the furniture except the silver? If your intention is to sell the goods, it must be at five percent so that we can bring in capital. But think? If you come to stay, will you find what you are looking for? We would have to buy land in the country. What we do with Mary? Do you still want to come?"*

Madame was too shrewd to let his anger grow. She wrote again, saying she wanted very much to come. Life without him was empty. She longed for his love.

When Stephen wrote again it was to the wife he adored: *"I think day and night about seeing you. I kiss you a thousand times. Kiss Mary for me. If you need anything, I ask Mary to get it for you and the same goes for her. I have nicely furnished the apartment for 1000 gourdes...Nicely furnished, beautiful bedroom with a view of park a l'Anglais...Servants quarters, root cellars, stables,*

106

cellar-laundry, wood cellar. Here you have a place for you whenever you come. I am your faithful husband forver."

But in January of the following year, Madame was still living in New York. She asked Stephen to send Mary a harp and a piano.

He was agreeable. *"I shall charge myself to get those instruments and send them to New York. I see you have the intention to keep St. Stephen. Is that for Mary's support? I don't know yet your decision to come back to France...My intention is to end my life in France. I can't tell you to come back. But think. I can't help to have oppressive thoughts of what you are doing...Neither do I want to tell you to sell the country estate. Once sold, you will never have a property to equal that. Think of that...I leave you mistress of all. Do as you like. My thought is always of Mary and her mother."*

In March the Atlantic separated them still. Stephen wrote wearily: *"I see you think of me. I can assure you I do the same. There isn't a minute when I don't think of you. I couldn't force you to come. You like the United States; and I, I don't like to cross the ocean. Otherwise I can live anywhere.*

I see you have leased the farm. You owe me 300 gourdes and M. Desorby 350. I find you have leased it too cheaply; but it is better that way, than to work it yourself. There is always enough produce for you to buy from your neighbor. I think you have enough hay from the forty acre river property in the north. One cow, pigs, enough milk and butter for you two. Desorby will give you enough for the maintenance of the property. You have to do your best to stay within limits. What for you plant grape vines? You just need grapes to eat. That is enough. They will only be stolen. I remember well how they stole them when I lived in New York. If it is your intention to stay, you must not make any more expenditures.

I can't give you the property of M. Durand.
Having his rent money will help your expenses. 15,000
gourdes. With that it is possible to live in the country. It
is not necessary for you to have company because all
visitors cost money. I am expecting your news and
especially those from Mary. I send her all the best."

Four months later he wrote: *"My dear Eliza, I*
have received your letter and Mary's. I am delighted that
your health is good. Yet Mary tells me you suffer from
migraine headaches. For that reason, you must not worry.
I am afraid it is only your_____. I know you very well.
It is possible that you are reacting to the thrift I am
teaching you. But it is a necessity. Business is very bad. I
have to advise you since I cannot do otherwise, and
remind you more than ever to economize. You may have
necessities, but no luxuries such as you had in the past.
Truly, it is impossible.

M. Durand tells me what I always fear about the
merchandise. Let's not talk about that again. It's better
not to do anything. I have no idea of what you say M.
Desorby has told you. I am sure you misunderstood him.
But better not to talk about it.

I miss Mary. She wrote me that she and her mother
were in New York to ask for the house of M. Durand. M.
Desorby has orders from me to rent that house; and the
rent money is for your expenses. These are the orders I
gave M. Desorby and he can't change that and let you
occupy the house. You should get 18,000 gourdes rent, and
with that sum you should live in style and decency. That
is what I want. If you think what it costs me to keep Mt.
Stephen! I do what I can to keep from working folly. We
will have to share to be able to live.

Truly, for four years I have eaten off my capital,

because for four years I haven't made any money. I beg you not to tell anyone this. One has to get by as best one can. I am at an age when I can't cross the ocean anymore. You can live quietly on Mt. Stephen. I know well that you love that retreat. With God's will, you will have everything you need there.

Tell Mary to keep on writing me in French. It is very good. She tells me I forget my English. That is the truth. For two years, I haven't spoken it at all."

Madame schemed to control the house rented by M. Durand because she needed the Mansion as bait. She had a quixotic new ambition, to enter that French society which had formed around the Emperor's brother Joseph. He had evaded the mousetrap at Rochefort and run the British blockade in an American vessel. He was warmly received in New York, and that summer, moved form the Astor House to a pretty little village on the Hudson River just below Harlem Heights. Madame thought to relive the drama of Rochefort, to offer her Mansion to Joseph, as she had to the Emperor.

She wrote listing her Bonaparte treasures, suggesting that he live on Mt. Stephen. He answered three times, refusing her offer curtly but courteously. *"Madame:"* he wrote for the last time, *"I am sorry for all the trouble you have taken in sending me lists of furniture and your kind offers of your beautiful country estate. But I have decided not to leave my estate in New Jersey. I can only reply by thanking you again and renewing my compliments."*

She had miscalculated. Joseph had fallen in love with his exquisite Quaker mistress. This was the happiest period of his life; and he was building his lover a palace on the Delaware River.

Nevertheless, he left a memory for Madame to distort and treasure. *"Joseph Bonaparte,"* she said when she was old, *"came to this country to marry me. He knew of my wealth and my European reputation...He lived in Manhattanville just to be near me and every day he drove up to see me. In fact, he bored me so much that I had to keep the gates locked against him. To my surprise, one day when I was out, he climbed over my fence and went to my kitchen where he ate pork and cabbage with my servants.*

To wipe out that bad treatment, I gave a great banquet." She said she had the doors of the dining room widened for that meal so that she, in her great skirt, could enter on his arm. *"The King,"* she said, *"was kind enough to compliment me on the elegance of my table."*

As a young whore, she had chosen the name Capet, and the royal dream grew more urgent. At forty-two, she was still waiting for a prince to recognize her, to elevate her to her rightful place. She had long since chosen that place, the throne of France. Nothing in those catastrophic years of revolution and restoration mattered. In her pantheon Bourbons and Bonapartes were interchangeable, for the French throne was only a symbol of that supreme station where she could reign above everyone who had ever humiliated or abused her.

The morés she adopted with middle age were compatible with her dream. A princess inspired desire but was herself transcendent. If a man designated as prince, failed to offer Madame a throne, his attentions became "tedious." Joseph "bored" her. And still the banquet she gave for him joined her fondest memories, for even in exile, he was forever King of Spain.

110

17

"Our sense of power is more vivid when we break a
man's spirit than when we win his heart."
Eric Hoffer

That fall Stephen suffered the financial failures
he had dreaded with all his faculties. *"I've had bad news
from New York."* He wrote. *"But let's not go into that.
But the House of Bordeaux informs me that we owe
100,000 francs. The House of Martinique wants the same
sum. Neither one knows what it will be able to return. I
won't hide it from you. This year is terrible. I have to
stay with my family in order to spend no more. I have to
be patient and wait and see what my losses will be. Never
write by way of Bordeaux. That way is too expensive...I
am without news of you."*
There were more princes in Paris than in New
York and Madame decided to join her husband. She
sold her more casual acquisitions. The paintings which
had hung in layers in her two great halls were put on
the auction block in April 1821. *"Original paintings
from Italian, Dutch, Flemish and French masters, selected
by the best Judges fom the Most Eminent Galleries in
Europe, intended for a Private Gallery in America,"* were
sold to the highest bidder.
Shortly thereafter Madame rented Mt. Stephen
to a family called Field, and after almost five years of
separation sailed for France to live with her husband.
Whatever the circumstances of their recon-
ciliation, the Jumel's were briefly reunited in an
apartment in the Place Vendome. From the letters of
shopkeepers, milliners and seamstresses, it is plain that

Madame would not or could not curb her extravagance. She soon resumed her place in society; aided again by the Countess de la Pagerie, who, as she had before, shared their apartment. Stephen was never included in the invitations Madame received. He stayed with his family, close to his business in Bordeaux. Sometimes the invitations included hapless Mary who at twenty had never been courted.

Whatever the Jumels suffered in private, Madame resumed her friendships with titled women as if she had never been away. Only the names are different: the Marquise de Veron, the Countess de Hartpoul, the Baroness de'Agilly, the Marquise de Maldieu, the Countess de Loyaulte de Loyaulte, the Marquis de Suze...widows, as useless and lonely as herself. She treasured their letters.

"I have the promise of two tickets for six o'clock for you and Miss Mary, and besides, a cavalier whom you will find most agreeable and who will be delighted to accompany you."

"We have just learned, Madame, that the King will go Tuesday to the Grande Opera in Richelieu Street. I hasten to tell you of it, for the boxes are very quickly sold out as soon as this news is known in society."

"A thousand regrets, my lady, for not being able to accept your kind invitation, but a previous promise keeps me from that pleasure."

In 1824, Louis XVIII died and his brother, the Count d'Artois was crowned. Madame attended the coronation in a yellow satin gown which took its place among her royal souvenirs.

Like Bonapartes and Bourbons, Madame's titled friends were interchangeable, and her only intimate, the Marquise de Suze, cared more for Madame's soul than her company. The Marquise's interest in her friend's salvation was intense. In spite of her conversion by desire, Madame was Catholic only at her convenience. She confessed her sins. The Marquise had stumbled on some unsavory aspect of Madame's past. Madame, turning to her in a moment of despair said, *"God help me."* In a moment of pride, she revealed the name of a famous lover. The Marquise, who lived in l'Abbaye aux Bois, wrote often.

"If your health is better, dear friend, I advise you to go hear a good sermon, which would please our good Abbe. There is a priest who has a fine reputation, at the Madeline, Rue St. Honore. Go there Sunday, if you can. He preaches at Vespers which will not interfere with your dinner hour... More than one friend of your little angel Mary, would like to see her more fervent in her faith. Always count on the sincerity of my feeling for you."

"How grateful I am to the good Abbe for going to see you. Yes, surely, every door in my house will be open to you, as well as to him. How good God is to have granted the continual and fervent prayers I have made for the eternal welfare of your soul."

Again: *"I shall not abandon the task I have begun and which I pray with fervor to complete. In His goodness and pity, I hope He will not make me endure such a grief. In all of this I am only seeking His glory and your present and future happiness. I do hope He will have mercy on us and will inspire you with the same hope for which I pray in every petition."*

Madame did not welcome God's attention. The demands of her friend seemed more like a shark smelling blood than a saint offering hope.

The Marquise's letters end in cold anger: *"So, you are going to make a long journey, Madame, and the great work which has so completely absorbed me and should have been still more absorbing to you must come to a standstill."*

Madame made a long journey. She joined her husband in the south of France; moved to that prominence in the flatland of Bordeaux called Mt. de Marsan where nothing at all roused her interest. Stephen loved her still. He counted on her loyalty and ability to save him from the quicksand of his businesses. They agreed to separate, but amicably, so that as his agent in America she could help him recoup his losses. They had an understanding, more meaningful to both of them than the formalities of marriage. They called it their "covenant". Madame was a divided woman. In part she believed in their covenant, and in part she saw Stephen's financial ruin and physical aging as a betrayal too profound to forgive.

Stephen would live in Bordeaux, Madame in America, at least until she had prepared the way in New York. M. Desorby, with his family, visited the Jumels in France. Stephen announced his retirement. Desorby bought his interest in their partnership. The larceny Stephen had committed against the House of Jumel & Desorby haunted him still. Certain phrases in his letters referred to his distress: *"If it had been my intention to run away... You know my motive, you were a witness... I am sure you misunderstood, but better not talk about it... There is more to say, I am afraid..."* Only someone who knew his secret could be trusted to manage his affairs. He trusted Eliza, his wife of twenty-two years.

Had it been otherwise, he would not have given her his power of attorney. That document, as much an instrument of trust as his marriage papers had been is poignant.

"Stephen Jumel, by power of attorney bearing the date May 15, 1826, constituted and appointed Eliza Brown Jumel his attorney to transact and manage his affairs at New York, and for him and in his name and for his use and in his behalf to sell either by public auction or private contract as she shall see fit and best for the price or prices that can be had or gotten, and for his behalf and advantage, all or any part of the real estate that he may have belonging to him and lying in the state of New York, and on sale thereof, or of any part thereof, to sign, seal and execute all and every such receipt of the monies arising from such sale or sales, to give sufficient release, acquitance and discharges for the same.

And I do hereby authorize and empower the said Eliza Brown Jumel...with such power or powers as to her shall seem meet and requisite and generally to do all things for the better executing of the premises as fully and in every respect as I might or could do if I were personally present...

In witness whereof, I have set my hand and seal, this fifteenth day of May in the Year of our Lord, one thousand, eight hundred and twenty-six. Stephen Jumel I.s. Signed, sealed and delivered in the presence of R. J. Macy, j.f.m., A.G. Barnet."

18

"A woman is a monster, and thank Heaven, an almost
impossible and hitherto imaginary monster, without
man as her acknowledged principle."
Nathaniel Hawthorn

Madame and Mary sailed for New York in May,
and since the mansion was occupied, rented a house for
the summer on Long Island. Stephen waited with
anguish for the money she had promised to send. He
wrote that he had been forced to sell twelve 'couvertes'
to pay his rent, and that he had discovered a new debt
of 8,000 gourdes. *"Be good enough then for the love of
God to send money to me at the old firm of J & D with the
running account."*

Madame answered affectionately, but her
warmth was maternal and she wrote as if to a child. In
a parody of his letters to her when their positions had
been reversed, she chided, advised and commanded as if
for his own good and on his behalf and for his benefit
and advantage.

A prostitute's sole advantage is to withhold
herself - to deceive her client with simulated
satisfaction. So, Madame, the old prostitute, simulated
the satisfaction of Stephen's need, always promising to
send him money, always withholding that money. She
had found the perfect antidote to loneliness and
boredom. The clarity and zest of her letters is
testament to the delight she took in the world of
business.

"I hope this letter will bring you back to New York

in the spring." she wrote. *"I think you can come in perfect safety. Mr. Hoffman advises you to come, but fearing he might not be a friend, I also applied to Mr. Kent. He tells me all the papers were destroyed. There is no danger, and since the property was not seized, and it is such a long time since the affair, that this is proof that no one believes it. Mr. Kent said that if he were in your place he would return, for you take no risk..."*

"If you come to New York and by chance anyone speaks to you about it, deny it flatly. Say the whole story is false - that it is an imposition. So, dear Stephen, make all your arrangements, for in the spring, I shall expect you."

"One day when Mr. Isreal was out, I made them give back all the old ledgers and books of our old association. The box was nailed up, and without doubt, no one has ever seen it...That man is half asleep and would never have the curiosity or interest to look inside. I opened it and found the letters from B.D. (Benjamin Desorby)."

"In looking through your papers, I've found those bearing on the schooner Prosper. There seems reason to hope the French government will reimburse us with interest...One must make a declaration before the month of September. "I have done everything in my power to procure money for you. But it is impossible. But since we have a house and furniture at Mt. de Marsan, wouldn't it be better to sacrifice that? Rather than what we have for our old age?"

"I've heard from persons who know what they are talking about that the Hartford bridge has been paying from ten to twelve percent for three years, while you are getting seven. If you haven't confidence enough in me to give me power of attorney for the Hartford Bridge, I beg you to choose another agent."

117

"Don't fail to give me next time the amount of the sum you received for the Mansion House, as well as the forty acres which have been let to Mr. Parsons, as well as from Cherry Valley and Courtland. Afterwards I will straighten my account with him."

"If you have any particular news, Monsieur, I beg you to address my letters to Mr. Workmeister. I don't fail to go to New York every day to watch over our affairs. I am most the active and best agent you've ever had because I am guided by your interests and mine which are identical, and I promise you, I neglect nothing. If you have orders to give me, I will execute them faithfully. I won't do as those wretches did."

"On thinking it over, I find the ides of our living together at the Mansion offers much happiness for old age. But I leave it to you to decide... Much love from Mary, who is getting remarkably stout. I am always hoping for the pleasure of seeing you. Farewell, dear Stephen. Take care of yourself. Eliza."

In October, she wrote: *"I am very flattered that you think of me; and at the same time I am sorry that you suffer penitence. You are wrong to stay home so much. If you should be ill, just imagine my despair. I did everything I could to procure you money. But it would be necessary to take out loans..."*

In November: *"Do you think you will spend the winter in Dieppe? But I am afraid you have given yourself too much trouble. It would have been better to sell the furniture than to rent the house, because really, my dear Stephen, you are in need of rest and should not worry about such things.*

"Mr. Brunel completely refuses to sell the stock in the Hartford bridge without a letter of authorization. There were very many good opportunities to get rid of the

stock, but unless you specify that I will send the money to you, it can't be done."

"I would have gone to the church and claimed the money for the articles you sent them, but first you have to send me a letter with the order. Otherwise, I'm afraid it's useless. Be assured that I will take care of our rights and our debts. Really, I don't see how I can procure money for you without great sacrifices."

In December: *"Mr. Lathrop has looked into the accounts of Mr. Brunel and has found they are not right. But that man is so sharp, he has put all his accounts in order, falsified, so they will seem to be right. You see, everyone is out to cheat us, even those who have a reputation for probity. Therefore, do not trust anyone but Eliza, who is and always will be, your faithful and able wife."*

In January: *"My dear Stephen, it would be impossible to tell you how much I endure to get you the sums of which you have so much need. As soon as I received your letter, I left my room which I haven't left for six weeks for I have a terrible cold which seems fixed in my chest. Sick as I was I had myself taken to Mr. Philipson and used all my eloquence so that he would give me the sum you are asking. First he gave me hope. But after two or three days he came to tell me that M. Salle does not wish to lend the money, and then I realized there is no more hope. Everyone is out for himself and friendship does not count for much.*

"I went to Mr. Lathrop, asked if he would loan you $5000. He told me he could do better with his monies. Then I offered him all the revenue from the Hartford bridge for $40,000 and in case of accident, I promised him seven percent forever - until it comes to capital. He was on the verge of agreeing but then he called M. Brunel, who

119

came running to tell me it is impossible. I can do absolutely nothing with those shares."

"I have also offered to mortgage the property on the island of New York, but no one will take it. These properties grow more valuable annually. But if I can obtain the monies, they will be sent to you. Because I am so tormented for this sum on account of you, I cannot sleep nights. I think I would be capable of mortgaging the house on Broadway, although I have promised myself that I would not ever do this."

"And if I should do this, what would we live on? You have to think on that well. I only hope M. Lasparre will send his power of attorney to sell the shares in the Hartford bridge. M. Brunel received the first October payment in 1822 and makes no mention of it is his reports. He sold six of our shares to a Miss Desorby. And that is all that is left us, forty shares, although before this time forty-six was marked on the certificates."

"Dear Stephen, I have all hopes of making good our covenant, to make possible our shelter and refuge...Mr. Richard is coming in now. I have offered him my diamonds, even if I get only $20,000, in order to send you something."

In February: *"I have neither a horse nor carriage, not anything to go to town. I must take the Albany stage to Manhattanville. I begged Mr. Philipson to help me provide the $3,000. He has promised to do anything in his power, as far as it depends on him... I have offered Mr. Juhen five percent if he can find a buyer for our properties, in order to advance this sum of money for you. For myself, I do not have the power to mortgage."*

"I have a bad cold. The Albany stage petrifies me with cold, so I kiss you in haste. I have offered my diamonds to sell, but nobody wants to give me anything

for them. The dear God is my witness, I am doing everything in my power for you. "

Madame may have taken the Albany stage, but she was not long without horses... Shortly after her return to New York, she drove to the City where her animal slipped and fell in front of the shop of her neighbor, Stephen Knapp. He had come to the door to see the cause of the ruckus and called out to a friend, *"It's only Madame Jumel. "* Stung by 'only', she had gone to New Jersey, brought four matched grays and the next day, dressed spectacularly, she showed them off in every village between New York and the Heights.

In May she wrote: *"My dear Stephen, I haven't had any word from you since December. I am completely astonished. Is it to make me miserable that you torment me like this? If you have the slightest feeling for me, you must know in what despair I am because of your silence. How can you be so cruel as to worry me so?*

I was at Mr. Philipson's today, and he told me he has found someone to take over the estate of the Hartford bridge. It will be a great sacrifice. But there is no other way to get the sum you are asking for and I won't do anything until I get your response. He tells me it is altogether shameful that I must come to town in a horse-drawn public vehicle, and then to walk around on foot. He has offered me enough money to buy some horses, but I refused him, not wanting to be in debt to any man. Therefore, dear Stephen, come back.

As soon as you have money enough to pay your debts, I beg you to come to America - to pass happy days in your pretty country house. Our little income will be enough if we live together. Separately, we cannot. Although I have neither a coachman nor a cook, and I do all the work myself, I see well by the expenses I have, that we cannot.

It would be better if you were here and we might recover our covenant. Think, my dear Stephen, you are not young anymore. You need care and who could give it to you better than your loving Eliza? I would do anything in my power to make you happy. Our differences might be forgotten. And we will live for one another, one for the other.

The grapevines are in flower, and it seems that we shall have many grapes since we have six hundred vines. I have cleared them well and they are well arranged. You would very much enjoy seeing them. And as for the garden, you cannot imagine how beautiful it is. The avenue and the surroundings are so well kept, it is like a paradise.

Thus to the best of her ability, she explained, confessed that the love she felt for her land was compulsive. But she included him. By invoking his presence in her vineyards, in her fashion, she asked forgiveness. She had reason to be frightened by his silence. Stephen could revoke his power of attorney. At very least, he could make a will leaving the Hartford bridge, Mt. de Marsan, and his free New York holdings to his relatives in Bordeaux.

Therefore, on the thirteenth of May, two weeks after writing that loving letter, Madame took steps to protect herself by hiring a lawyer. She chose her neighbor, Alexander Hamilton, II, son of Burr's great enemy. In a series of transfers, using her power of attorney, she had all of Stephen's holdings put in trust for Mary, reserving the revenue for herself. When these transactions were finished, Stephen Jumel had neither property in New York, nor income from anything that had been his. She controlled everything in Mary's name, "as if," and these words are on every document, "she were a femme sole."

Yet, when she heard from Stephen again, she wrote as she had before; scolding him for his thoughtlessness and saying that she would send money when she could.

"Finally I received your letter of the thirteenth. As M. Brunel lives on South Street, I do not like to go to this part of the City. It is dedicated to the commerce of women. Ladies do not go there. In the future, I beg you to send letters to Mr. Workmeister. Be sure I will do everything in my power to get money and you will know the results of my efforts in my next letter. Adieu, my dear Stephen. Believe me, forever your affectionate wife. Eliza"

Stephen arrived in New York in the summer of 1828, humiliated, exhausted and dependent. He had made no will. He was content that the accumulations of his life and Madame's become Mary's insurance.

Madame and her daughter went South for the winter. He sought the company of his wife's servants. *"James,"* he said to Madame's coachman, *"I didn't give Eliza that paper to rob me with."*

James answered compassionately. *"Mr. Jumel, I knew that fact when it was done."*

As old people must, Stephen reviewed his life; and as memories compelled attention, present wrongs poisoned what pleasure he might have taken in the past. He was oppressed with a sense of failure.

Madame, whose actions sprang from motives beneath the level of thought, suffered no shame. She presented herself as she had in her letters, as his benevolent wife. To insure Stephen's comfort in his old age, and to provide for herself and Mary it had been necessary to make good his failure. He was fortunate that she had had the energy and ability to make it so. Many people prefer to live in their ego's consciousness, to justify its craving for pleasure and power; and the energy necessary to sustain the ego's fictions is a measure of the force of its craving. So it was with Madame.

Mary, who by her presence had once caused violent scenes between her parents, still acted as buffer; and the masks they wore for her sake, hid what they felt as victor and victim in their covenant.

But Mary was not a source of happiness. She was as helpless as an infant. Madame had never recognized her as an individual in her own right, and she had never so seen herself. She trusted Madame to make life easy and to protect her from adversity. Her sole pleasure was eating. At thirty she was soft and corpulent, shielded by fat from the attentions of men.

To be a spinster was to be branded unwanted. Madame could not tolerate social disdain. Disingenuously she took Mary with her to Worcester, where she visited Judge Crispin, ostensibly to consult him about matters of real estate, but really to introduce Mary to the Judge's assistant, Nelson Chase. Chase's bright black eyes and slender build reminded Madame of Burr. Others spoke of the resemblance. Chase was attentive to Mary and deferential to Madame. Seeing that he was aware of his advantage, Madame made the proposal. *"I see there is friendship between you and Miss Mary,"* she said. *"If you and she can agree, I should be happy to have you as my son-in-law."* She cared little about the outcome. If Chase accepted, he was malleable. If his pride was stiff, he would not do. He

124

had none.

Madame spelled it out. She would support the household. In return the Chases would be expected to make their home with her. At her death, Madame was emphatic, Mary would be her sole heir, and as Mary's husband, Nelson Chase would thus be custodian of her fortune. Madame left Mary in Judge Crispin's household so that the engaged couple could become acquainted. Mary agreed to stay three months.

Madame did not hide from herself the wretched prospect of living alone with Stephen and before she left Worcester, she found and adopted another child, eight-year-old Mary Steever, whose parents agreed to let her live with Madame for an indefinite period. The homesick child became Madame's shadow. As Mary Steever would testify, she slept in Madame's room. They had breakfast together on the balcony and supped together at five. Once a day, the miserable family met in the dining room where Stephen appeared for a formal meal.

Madame had never come to terms with the dark side of her nature, that narcissistic inner infant who felt its need so fiercely. As Freud said, the infant loves itself with supreme egotism; and when the resources of adulthood are used without the inner controls of adulthood, the resultant behavior is likely to be deplorable. Madame's strength had its roots in such an ego. It was her great strength as a courtesan; it made her an incisive business woman. But her hidden infant was unregenerate, undisciplined and potentially criminal.

19

"Since that event which separated me from the human
race, I have been able to neither give nor receive
comfort."
Aaron Burr

When Burr slipped back to New York, he was
fifty-six. He had come to the City by stealth and
hidden in the room of a prostitute. He was wanted for
murder and afraid of debtors' prison. Nevertheless, on
the eight of June, 1812, hoping that neither the law nor
his creditors would prosecute him, he paid for an
advertisement to run in New York papers: *"Colonel
Aaron Burr has returned to New York to resume his
practice at law."* The news swept the city. In the first
twelve days of his practice he made $12,000. Then his
heart turned to Theodosia and his grandson. He wrote
to her joyfully about the future.

Theodosia answered his joyful letter telling him
that her son was dead. *"My child is gone forever. May
Heaven by other blessings make you amends for what you
have lost. I think Omnipotence could give me no
equivalent for my boy. No. None..."*

His son-in-law's letter followed. *"Theodosia has
endured all that a human being could endure. She
supports herself in a manner worthy of your daughter...
My present wish is that she should join you. I not only
recognize your claim to her after such a separation, but
change of scene and your company will aid her."*

Burr sent his physician to his stricken daughter,
and escorted by him, she boarded a vessel called the
Patriot, which was expected in New York within six

days. A storm of dreadful violence swept up the coast and the Patriot vanished. No one aboard was ever heard from again.

Anguished letters passed between Burr and his son-in-law. "*Wretched, heart-rendering forebodings distract my mind. I may no longer have a wife. Gracious God, why am I preserved?* And: *"Thirty days is decisive. My wife is either captured or lost."*

Burr ceased to mourn Theodosia only with his life. But he was able to act on his principles He went about his daily business with composure. He was not tortured by hope. *"She is dead. If she were alive, no power on earth would keep her from coming to me."*

Tragedy made him compassionate rather than bitter. Although he pursued the law as before, he seemed to conduct himself with benign indifference. He was more spendthrift than ever. Every morning he emptied his pockets of all he had, leaving the money inside a wall of books arranged on his law table. His door was always open. Anyone was free to help himself.

Burr kept no account of his largess. He provided firewood for freezing families and supported old veterans. He kept an alcoholic lawyer through his dying years. His tenderness for the young was excruciating. At this time in his life he paid for the education of at least a dozen young people. *"He worked,"* said Colonel Craft, *"twenty-four hours a day."*

For several years he lived with the Widow Eden and acted as a legal guardian to her two daughters. When all three married and departed, the Widow Blodgett appealed for help, reminding him that her heart had never been estranged from his. He gave her the money he could not win for her in court and took her son into his law office. Although it was not his natural condition, he was living alone, when Madame Jumel approached his desk to ask for legal advice.

She prepared herself with trepidation, exquisitely aware that he had not seen her for more than thirty years; that he remembered her, if he did, as a very young woman. With all the art in her command she swung her huge skirts through the door of his office at 23 Nassau and saw that the advantage was hers. She was twenty years his junior.

He rose to the occasion like a fish to a fly; as gallant as Madame was hungry for gallantry.

This letter from Mary Hassals, who had written to help, suggests the loyalty Burr could inspire in an old mistress. *"O, I knew this hour would come. In my dreams I have beheld you looking benignly on me; and something whispered in my heart that at length the hour, fraught with feeling, would be given me, that again in your presence, I should feel that unmixed delight which from you only I have received - that happiness attending the most pure, ardent, most exalted friendship..."*

So had he won the friendship of Madame Jumel. He concentrated on the legal problem she brought him, an exercise carefully calculated to let him know that in her own right, as a femme sole, she was one of the richest women in the United States. When the interview ended, he handed her up to her yellow calash as if it were painful to let her go. Madame was not alone in thinking of Burr's courtesy as a caress.

She was intoxicated. The usual vision of glory rose from the ashes of old infatuation. She endowed him then with the mantle of the prince who would save her. In her hierarchy, Vice President was an equivalent title. Burr would share his name and, albeit former, rank with her, elevate her to her rightful place. The Vice Queen of America, so she would refer to herself.

When she played this game with Joseph Bonaparte, it had not mattered that Madame had a husband in Europe and Joseph a wife. This was a drama with a difference; she had found a prince who was willing to play his part.

Then as she weighed the small value Stephen's life had to him (a frail, bitter, dependent old man) against the great value his death would be to her, his existence seemed insupportable. She revived in her mind the old shame of his advances to Mary.

In May, when Stephen fell from a hay cart on Kings Bridge Road and was carried home suffering from concussion, the idea of his dying from the fall must have seemed to Madame like an omen and a gift. At her direction he was carried to a room on the third floor.

The third floor of the Mansion has a curious feature. Presumably to make it easier to put things in storage or retrieve them, every attic room has two doors which open into the space between the shell of the house and the walls of the rooms. Thus a low, hidden, circular hall encompasses the attic; furthermore, there is hidden access to this space from the floor below, a staircase in the closet of the corridor leading to the octagonal bedroom. Therefore, a person could enter or leave any room on the third floor secretly, without being seen in the halls or on the great stairs.

But if Madame wanted to visit Stephen's chamber secretly, she could not while Mary Steever slept beside her. That night in spite of torrential rain and lightening, which struck two churches in the city, Madame asked James to take Mary Steever to her mother's home in Worcester, a little town as far north as Albany and rather farther west. Before the household settled into its uneasy rest, Madame summoned a doctor who bled Stephen. Bleeding was a common, harmful, but seldom fatal treatment for most injuries and diseases.

Sometime in the night Stephen bled to death. His blood ran out under the door of his room, across the landing where the floor slopes, to fall free of the stairs, making a ghastly pool on the floor of the great hall three flights below.

A Grand Jury indicted Madame for murder. But the case was dismissed without trial.

Forty-eight years later, questioned by Bowen's lawyer, about the night when Stephen died, Mary Steever said she did not know why she had been sent away. She was asked if, in connection with that night, Madame said she had committed a sin. Bowen's lawyer objected. When he was an old man, Colonel Craft, Burr's law partner, told his physician that "*across the proceedings clearing the way for the marriage (of Eliza and Burr) lay the shadow of a crime.*" He said Stephen bled to death from a lancet wound. Whether he guessed or whether he knew cannot be ascertained. Nor do the City archives yield further information.

Stephen's obituary was terse. *"Died: Stephen Jumel, Esquire at his home in Harlem Heights on Monday last, May 22, 1832."*

The rain continued. It rained when his coffin was committed to the earth in the cemetery of the old Cathedral on Prince Street, the church on which he had lavished gifts in gratitude for his marriage.

130

His tomb, once supported by four pillars, now rests on a crude brick platform. The marble has eroded in the polluted air. Only one who knows what to look for can trace the wasted letters and spell, half by sight and half by touch *S T E P H E N   JU M E L*. One can do as much for the donor's name at the foot of the monument, the letters are of equal size, *E L I Z A   J U M E L*.

Stephen's soul did not go gently. Spectral evidence of his agony lingered in the house. Rapping and other phenomena, which Madame attributed to his ghost, frightened her badly. His restless spirit made the house untenable. Imposing exile on herself, she moved to Greenwich Street in the City.

That September Nelson Chase and Miss Mary were married in Worcester. Mary was soon pregnant and fearing a miscarriage, the young couple moved to a house near Madame's to be near her French physician. She, belle mere sans merci, broke her lease and moved in with them. But even on Greenwich Street, with the young couple for protection, Madame found it hard to lay the ghost of her conscience.

In spite of that, she proceeded bravely. The apartment she rented was as convenient to Burr's office as to her physician's. The Colonel suggested that she send her son-in-law to receive his opinion on her deeds and indentures. Chase was a reluctant go-between. No story about Burr was too vile for public acceptance. It was said that he had hired pirates to sink the Patriot, drowning his daughter in order to hide his affair with the captain's wife. Chase assumed he had to deal with the most cunning and evil of men.

But he was overwhelmed by Burr's acuteness, his knowledgeability, and his extraordinary charm. Chase praised him to Madame and became an advocate

131

of their courtship. Burr told Chase he could teach him more in a year than he could learn anywhere else in ten, and offered him a position in his office. Dutifully Chase asked Madame's permission, and gracefully she gave it.

Once ensconced, Chase was shocked by his mentor's charity. *"Colonel Burr seems wholly to have lost the power to say no,"* he reported to Madame, *"although in no other way is he decrepit."* Chase pressed her to re-introduce Burr to society. Possibly the irony of this struck neither Chase nor Madame Jumel; for in the public mind, Burr was still anathema, a lecher, a murderer and a traitor.

In January Mary bore a stillborn child. With the coming of spring there was no ostensible reason to remain in the City. Urged by Chase, and following her own inclination to receive Burr's attention among her own dear trophies, Madame led her entourage back to the Heights. She dealt with Stephen's ghost physically. She had joists tightened, beams re-enforced, and squeaking boards re-laid; as if it would be more difficult then for Stephen to make his presence known. She armed herself, so that at any time when she was confronted by a frightening phenomenon, she could pick up a pistol; presumably not to shoot Stephen's spirit, but to remind him that in life she had faced him with a pistol and he had given way. Finally, she sent to Worcester for Mary Steever, and the child slept beside her as she had before. Madame's visceral intelligence reassured her, and she came to feel that those remnants of Stephen's misery which haunted the house were no more awful than his physical presence had been.

20

"I learn with pleasure that my soul is dearer to you
than my body, and that your good sense leads you as
always to the better part."
Ninon de Lenclos

For Burr, too, the Mansion was filled with
ghosts. Driving in a hired hack up to that house, he
was driven back to his youth; cold Washington, craven
Leffingwell, brave Hale, obsequious Hamilton...to
himself as a gallant young officer. The Theodosia's
approbation was bittersweet. *"How many delightful
walks can be made on one hundred and thirty acres. How
much of your taste displayed. It would be a principality.
There is for me something stylish, elegant, respectable and
suitable for you to have such a handsome country seat."*
The banquet in his honor was magnificent. No
one refused Madame's invitation. Burr was a great
curiosity, the last of the founding fathers, the only
villain. As he gave Madame his arm, he murmured, *"I
offer you my hand Madame. My heart has always been
yours."*
Burr began to comfort the widow, to play whist
with her evenings, to drive with her in the afternoon.
He despised himself for courting Madame. He chose
the circumstances and the occasion of their marriage as
a suicide chooses an emotionally ladened anniversary,
to give meaning to his death. He celebrated the death
of love and honor, appreciating the symmetry of
himself as a whore, marrying a whore. He chose to
marry Madame Jumel on the fiftieth anniversary of his

marriage to Theodosia's beloved mother. In the same spirit of derision, he asked the same clergyman, the man who had joined him to his first wife, to perform the ceremony. Burr was seventy-eight. *"Madame,"* he said, *"I will bring a clergyman out to Washington Heights tomorrow evening and once more solicit your hand."*

He spoke in such a manner that Madame, doubting for a moment her commitment to the drama, retreated. *"My heart is faithful to the memory of M. Jumel,"* she said. Something about the impending marriage embarrassed her, and as if sex and death were equally unspeakable, she sent little Mary Steever back to Worcester.

That same night, while she could still sign herself Madame Jumel, she acknowledged a letter of condolence from Stephen's nephew in Bordeaux, the man who had held Stephen's power of attorney for his stock in the Hartford bridge. The sharpness of her hypocrisy had been honed on Stephen.

"To M. Lesparre Sante, Mt. de Marsan, France. My Dear nephew: It is always gratifying to hear eulogies of my dear departed husband, especially from one who had such a unique opportunity to assess his character and virtues. The desolation of my heart at the sudden loss of my husband and dear friend have disqualified me from the usual enjoyments of life.

My niece Mary, about who you have the goodness to inquire, was married a while ago to a gentleman whose profession is law and whose residence is in New York - and I take great comfort and solace in the society of my niece and her husband.

In reply to the inquiries which you have the goodness to make, respecting the affairs of m. Jumel, I might refer you to your recollection of the circumstance under which he left Europe. Since that period nothing has changed to improve his fortunes or to redeem the errors he suffered in France which so greatly impoverished him. The value of the whole property as it was appraised by the public authorities of the City, amounted to only four thousand dollars - and the debts which he owed in this country amounted to fifty thousand francs. Under these circumstances, I have been compelled to relinquish many of the comforts to which I had become accustomed. I therefore have no prospect of visiting France. I thank you for your very courteous offers of hospitality, as well as your great interest in my welfare, which I assure you is reciprocated by your affectionate aunt. Eliza Jumel."

Stephen died intestate and what properties he had retained, his shares in the Hartford bridge and whatever he still owned in Europe, automatically reverted to his widow. She had managed his affairs brilliantly for seven years, and her assets at the time of her second marriage lay between two and three million dollars. Burr had reason to think she would keep him in comfort.

He kept his word. The following evening he drove up to Harlem Heights with the Reverend David Bogart, but when his carriage rolled through the bowed gates, Madame ran upstairs in a frenzy of coyness. Her reluctance was real. Age and atrophy had restored her psychic virginity and she was afraid. Coyness suited her mythology. Madame's princess found the marriage bed distasteful, but she would sacrifice herself. Madame's game that night was as strange as Burr's.

"Chase caught me on the landing," she said, *"and prayed me to marry Colonel Burr. He said he would be ruined if I did not; that Burr would turn him out of his office. He said the Colonel had promised him the deed to a*

135

village on the North River and would give him $150,000 from Trinity Church, which he would collect next week, if only I would marry Colonel Burr." This argument, which suggested how deeply Chase had become involved in Burr's affairs, gave Madame an excuse to submit to his suit. *"The poor boy appealed to my sympathy,"* she said. *"And I ran downstairs to where Burr was standing at the foot. He caught my hand and dragged me with him to the parlor, saying the minister was old and it was close to midnight-"* when Burr's sacred anniversary expired. *"And he was so brave and fine,"* she said, *"that like a fool, I took his hand and married him."*

Madame, who was not unprepared, provided the wedding supper. The party was merry, if only because each member of the wedding believed the ceremony was to his financial advantage, except the Reverend Bogart, who giddy with wine talked about events long passed and persons long dead. They were all wrong, Chase's gift from his mentor was two mahogany chairs, the last of Burr's property from Richmond Hill.

New Yorkers were amused at the union of the two old lovers. Philip Hone wrote in his celebrated diary: *"The celebrated Colonel Burr and the equally celebrated Mrs. Jumel, widow of Stephen Jumel, were married Wednesday, July 3. It is beneficent of her to keep him in his latter days. One good turn deserves another."*

136

21

"She was a devil incarnate, overbearing and domineering beyond human endurance."
Colonel William D. Craft

Madame's narrow Bonaparte bed would not accommodate two, nor did she wish to share it. Formally Burr would occupy the room across the hall, but he would be sexually active until a stroke paralyzed his lower body.

He knew that Madame possessed the Mansion wholly. The walls were papered with her pretensions. Every letter she had ever received from a titled person was framed and hanging. Her emblem, the eagle with the body of a quiver, hung over the arch in the hall. Her paintings were chosen in a similar vein of self-tribute. He smiled at the vanity of her associations: Romeo and Juliet, Romulus and Remus, Antony and Cleopatra, a full-length portrait of Washington, Napoleon as Caesar bestraddling the world...Her vanity was omnipresent.

A few days after the ceremony, the Burrs began their wedding journey with a trip to his eminent relatives in Connecticut. His nephew, the governor received them cordially. Then, without argument, Burr accomplished what the anguished letters of Stephen Jumel could not, the sale of the stock in the Hartford bridge. According to family tradition, the purchaser offered $6,000 to Madame, who grandly waved it aside. *"You must give the money to my husband, Colonel Burr."* Burr sewed the prodigious packet of bills in his coat pocket; and when the honeymoon was over, deposited them to his own account in the Bank of Manhattan.

Madame knew of Burr's scheme to settle Texas with German emigrants and advanced this sum to advance his scheme. He had once plotted to make his daughter Queen of Mexico. He let Madame see herself as Queen of Texas. He did not tell her that his agent in Texas was his great friend, Jane McManus. He told Chase that time had justified his western adventure. *"What was treason thirty years ago is patriotism now,"* he said. Fortunes were to be made in Texas, but not by Burr. His plan was an unmitigated disaster. All of Burr's money and that part of Madame's were, in effect, thrown away.

She demanded an accounting. Burr, who sometimes found it convenient to sleep in his office, sent an answer back by Chase. *"Tell her it is no affair of hers. And will you please remind the lady she has a husband to manage her affairs now, and that he intends to do it."*

When he came home Madame drove him from the house with fire tongs. He moved to a boarding house on Duane Street; and Chase, always protective of his inheritance, told Madame that Burr could make inroads in her fortune unless she divorced him.

But divorce was not accepted in society. In Madame's view, it was essential that they appear to live on good terms. She begged him to come home. Much to the distress of Colonel Craft who despised her, she apologized. She said she had spoken in haste. Burr was pleasant; he called her his Madame of the Heights, but he would not live with her.

The only amiable interest she shared with Burr, but could not, was a fondness for children. In that first lonely year of her second marriage, she projected herself into the lives of the Wallace twins who were born next door. She asked permission to name them. The should be named for her husbands, Stephen Jumel and Aaron Burr. Jacob Wallace told Madame that he wouldn't call the dogs in his yard such names. The twins were christened Alexander Hamilton and Stephen Hamilton.

But when Burr refused to live with her, the name Hamilton no longer offended. She was, in fact, pleased and sent to Germany for a box of toys. It was her pleasure to see that the twins were dressed in identical clothes; and when they were older, they played in her yard as if it were an extension of their own.

Burr continued his practice. This description was written by a young man, new to the City: *"Burr was pointed out to me...slowly winding his way up Broadway, between Chambers Street and the Old Theater. He was small, thin and attenuated in form, perhaps a little over five feet in height, weight not over a hundred pounds. He walked with a slow measured step, stooping considerably, occasionally with both hands behind his back. Small, wrinkled face; keen, deep-set eyes. His hat set deep on his head, the back part sunk down on the collar of his coat, and the black brim somewhat turned upwards. Dressed in threadbare black cloth, having the appearance of what is known as shabby genteel. His countenance wore a melancholy aspect. His whole appearance betokeneth one dejected, forsaken or cast aside - and conscious of his position.*

He was invariably alone when I saw him, except on the single occasion that was on the sidewalk of Broadway, fronting what is now the Astor House, standing talking familiarly with a young woman whom

139

he held by the hand. His countenance on that occasion was cheerful, lighted up, bland; altogether different from what it appeared to me when I saw him alone in conversation with himself. In looking at this fragment of humanity, it appeared mysterious to me that he could have become famous in history or noted for good or bad actions of any sort."

Toward the end of 1833, Burr suffered his first stroke. He was stricken in the street and carried to his office. Madame went to him immediately and carried him back to the Heights where he lay in the front parlor in front of the fire, on a couch which had allegedly belonged to Napoleon.

Burr's recuperative powers were strong, but his incompatibility with Madame was elemental. At the end of five weeks he left her again to share the rooms of a jeweler who claimed to be his son, Aaron Columbus Burr. Burr had paid for the boy's education, as he paid for the education of any young person, male or female, who claimed paternity. In that apartment, Aaron Columbus painted the quizzical, gentle last portrait of Colonel Burr; and had lithographs made to hawk in anticipation of his father's death.

A mutual acquaintance, meeting Madame on Broadway, asked about Burr's health and she poured out an account of the money he had lost. *"He got $13,000 of my property and spent it all or gave it away. I had a carriage and a pair of horses which cost me over a thousand dollars and he took them and sold them for five hundred."*

What confidence can be put in the words of a woman like that, I do not know," wrote the gentleman. *"And what can I not believe of Burr for marrying her!"*

She sued for divorce; and meaning to hurt him, as far as that was in her power, she recalled the son of Alexander Hamilton to act on her behalf. Custom required the testimony of two witnesses willing to swear that they watched the defendant commit adultery. With the righteousness of a reformed whore, she went beyond custom and said that Burr's lewd and polluted habits had so endangered her health that she was compelled to live apart from him. Burr had suggested acts, which in the fullness of her knowledge she associated with prostitution, acts she believed no gentleman would suggest to his wife. Almost as an afterthought she added that he wasted her money to pay debts contracted before their marriage.

Maria Johnson, a half-witted black servant who worked for Burr, was hired to spy on her master. She swore she saw him make love to Jane McManus of Jersey City on a settee in the back room on the first floor of Jane's house. *"I got up on the shed and turned the window blind up and looked through...Then I set down on my hunkies and looked in. And Colonel Burr had his trousers all down and he had his hand under her clothes and I saw her nakedness. They were,"* she said in answer to a question, *"about as close together as they could get together. And I looked at them until they got through their mean act."*

One other occasion, Maria surprised them. *"I came upstairs to fetch Colonel Burr a pitcher of water...and I said 'Oh la! Mercy save us!' And Colonel Burr said he rang the bell accidentally."* He offered to buy Maria a pair of shoes to hold her tongue, but she was angry. As she told the court, *"I did tell and will tell and always meant to tell because it was Sunday, and I was ready to go to church, and he gave me orders to go to the*

Bear Market to get oysters for Jane McManus' dinner. "

Jane McManus moved to Texas.

The second witness, Doctor Ezekial P. Johnson, swore he too surprised Burr with Jane McManus in an act of unchastity. *"Burr,"* he said, *"in great agitation and with much warmth of expression told Maria Johnson never to permit the Doctor into his rooms without first sending him word. In the future, when the doctor called, he was to be seated in the front room. "*

Doctor Johnson moved to Mexico.

Burr let his lawyer answer in kind. He had hired Charles O'Conor, a tall man, known for his ability to inspire fear and confusion in a witness (who would be chosen by Nelson Chase to defend him against George Washington Bowen). O'Conor said, *"The vile and ferocious temper of the oratrix drove Burr from the house. "* Madame had been *"disobedient and insulting. "* He resurrected her name as a prostitute, if only obliquely, saying that he had discovered no more than four of her paramours: William B. Parson, Robert Covey, James Sommers, and Lawrence _____, Christian name unknown.

Burr asked permission to amend the list, adding the names of Charles Percy, Patrick Delehanty, and Charles Saunders. He said his list would be formidable except that he had been confined to his chambers except on two occasions when, he said, he had gone abroad for not more than an hour and each time with great difficulty.

During these squalid proceedings, Chase continued to work for Burr as his agent in Washington. Burr trusted Chase, as Stephen had trusted Eliza to act in good faith and for his benefit. But Chase had no probity, and mindful of his inheritance, betrayed his mentor to please his mother-in-law. The nature of Burr's project is as enigmatic as his letters.

"To Nelson Chase. January 20, 1834.

Permit me to say, I expect to receive a daily report of your doings in this particular matter stating what you have done or attempted to do each day, and what replies, encouragement or discouragement you expect or apprehend. Colonel O. is a man who expects to form his own judgment of facts presented to him. To write that you are in trouble, doubt or discouraged is of no use unless you tell us the causes. I write you as often as I have anything to say, a little oftener. My last, among other things, contained receipt of a draft for $45 on the Bank of Manhattan in your favor. When a letter containing money is not answered by return mail, the conclusion is that it has been stolen or lost, which gives rise to a double solicitude: first from the loss of money, and again that the correspondent, friend or agent addressed may be suffering from the want of it and cursing his principal. Salve.

God speed you. I wish you a happy New Year.

A. Burr."

"January 29, 1834.

Colonel O. complains very much of the bareness of your letters. We do not know whether further affidavits will be required.

God Bless and speed you.

A. Burr"

"February 1, 1834.

I give you carte blanche, but with this admonition. That it is a very difficult business and will not profit by any default. Take care how you conduct yourself. Examine well before you move. From another quarter, you will have something to aid you.

    Salve.

        A. Burr"

      "February 5, 1834.

No Letter has been received since yours of the 31st which communicated nothing. That of the 30th informed me that you had made the acquaintance of a gentleman of influence and consideration who was willing to assist you for a commission; the amount not named. But you are not pleased to give the name of the gentleman nor any clue to or indication of him. I have not now any instructions to give.

    Salve.

        A. Burr"

      "February 14, 1834.

Your letter of the 11th this morning received. If your judges have candor and intelligence, you are certainly in a good way, having overcome the principal, and as it seemed to me, the only remaining objection. Yet sophistry and malice may invent others. We regret very much that you did not deign to inform us who is Mr. Young, his country, his pedigree, his associations. Ditto of Mr. Cox. You mention no details or photographs, notwithstanding that I wrote you yesterday on the subject of finance.

    God bless and speed you.

        A. Burr"

      "May 17, 1834

Do me the favor to answer a letter which I wrote you more than a week ago requesting more precise information. How is Madame and the belle petite? Are you in town or

country? And where?
Salutem.

A. Burr"

In 1835 Burr suffered a second stroke which paralyzed him from the waist down leaving him helpless. Colonel Craft said many notable lawyers offered to defend him then in his counter suit for divorce. But Burr was sick of the sordid affair. Craft begged him to protect his reputation. *"For God's sake, no,"* Burr said. He abandoned his defense, allowing Madame's original bill to be taken pro confesso - removing the stigma from her name without regard for his own.

It is a measure of the meanness of Nelson Chase, that he chose this time to sue Burr for the loss of certain law books, *"in the amount of value of $300,"* which he claimed Burr had stolen.

Burr had withdrawn from things of this world and gathered his energies for death. An old friend took the paralyzed man into the basement of her boarding house. The Widow Webb was a romantic woman; when Burr first knew her she had been married to two men. Nevertheless, she had fallen in love with Burr and she worshipped him still.

Unhappily she was forced to sell her boarding house and Burr's cousin had the old man carried on a litter to a hotel on Staten Island. He was propped up so that he could look at the harbor and the ships riding at anchor.

"If only I could see her coming to me over the water." Burr wept as he spoke. Everyone knew he meant Theodosia. His last word was *"Madame."* He seemed to gesture with his eyes toward his spectacles.

No one thought he meant Madame Jumel, and his glasses were given to Madame Webb.

He slipped from life without resistance. That same day, September 14, 1836, Madame won her suit for divorce in the Court of Chancery. Burr was free of the furies that stalked him; and Madame was free to call herself either the widow of the Vice President of the United States, or his divorced wife, or, if she chose, Madame Jumel. The Court restored her name and title as if Burr had never lived.

She wept for him. Burr's biographer, James Parton, who interviewed Madame wrote: *"What is strangest of all, is that this lady, though she never saw her husband the last two years of his life, cherished no ill will. To this hour, Madame Jumel thinks and speaks of him with kindness, attributing what was wrong or unwise in his conduct to the infirmities of age."*

Burr's passing was mourned by those who loved him, but the public rejoiced. *"Thus passed from the scene one who might have been a glorious actor,"* said an editorial celebrating his death. *"And when he was laid in the grave, decency congratulated itself that the nuisance was removed. And good men were glad that God had seen fit to deliver society from the contaminating contact of a festering mass of moral putrification."*

22

"And on the highest throne in the world, we are sitting
on our own ass."
Montaigne

Maria Johnson, the feeble-minded   servant
whose testimony had been instrumental in winning
Madame's divorce, was charged with perjury by Burr's
relatives, whose concern for their good name took
precedence over the dead man's wishes. From the
wrath of the verdict it would seem, that had it been
within their power, the jury would have damned her to
hell.

*"The jurors of the people of New York, upon their
oath present that Maria Johnson, spinster, did wickedly
and maliciously, connivingly and intending unjustly to
aggrieve... And not having the fear of God before her eyes,
but being moved and seduced by the instigation of the
Devil, did commit willful and corrupt perjury against the
statute to the displeasure of Almighty God and the
contempt of the people of this State and of their laws."*
The man who might have protected her was, of course,
dead.

Almost coincident with Burr's death, was the
birth of little Eliza Jumel Chase. The death of two
husbands was compelling evidence of Madame's own
mortality. This surrogate, a grandchild, a physical
extension beyond the grave, pleased her. But she was
too self-centered to lose herself in the on-going life of
her family, too estranged from nature to wholly accept
the consolation of continuity. She longed to control
time as she did her household. She had set too high a

price on beauty to relinquish it gracefully and she dealt with the process of aging as she had with Stephen's ghost, with the bold use of physical props.

There is a description of Madame Jumel greeting old friends of Burr's (gentlemen who knew of Burr's death but not of her divorce) wearing a royal purple gown slit at the sides to show an embroidered underskirt of yellow satin. Old residents on the Heights remembered her entrances at the Church of the Intercession, her rusting taffeta, swinging hoops, trailing ostrich plumes and perfume. Father Smith, either in deference or in mockery, would stop the service until she was seated. Not only did she dress as the gaudy beauty she had been, she forced herself to move with grace and agility. When she was angry she still tossed her head and stamped her foot. And still, an old footman recollected, *"she wagged off."*

In the summer of 1835 she rented a house for herself and the Chases in the bohemian resort of Hoboken. She had tenuous connections. Her attorney, Alexander Hamilton II, was a member of the Township. Stephen's friend Bayard and Burr's friend Swarthout managed tenant farms. Madame's better in matters of foreclosure and indenture, John Jacob Astor, had a mansion on Castle Point. Washington Irving, Edgar Allen Poe, William Cullen Bryant, and the painter Thomas Cole, summered there. Perhaps a hundred houses were clustered along the one main street. Others stood apart like medieval manors. Hoboken had a medicinal spring, a fine restaurant, an embryonic railroad, a path along the Palisades, an avenue of elms, a willow walk; all places to see and be seen by those who wished to see and be seen.

In winter, when the Hudson was frozen and the

ferry seldom ran, Madame felt cut off. With or without the Chases, she moved to the Astor House.

Then, miraculously, history put another Bonaparte in Madame's way, another prince to wish on. Louis Napoleon, son of the Emperor's youngest brother, led an abortive coup d'etat against Louis Phillipe. He was arrested and without benefit of trial shipped to America. His uncle, Joseph Bonaparte, refused to receive him; and having limited resources, Louis rented a room on Bloomfield Street, Hoboken.

He seldom went out, except to walk to Castle Point. Occasionally with his friend the cigar maker, he ventured into the interior of New Jersey to shoot birds. In Europe his amorous reputation was Napoleonic. In Hoboken his conduct was impeccable. Those who met him were usually moved. He spoke so tenderly of his mother, the Queen; so sincerely about his right to be King. He was short, swarthy and hawk-nosed; but he had inherited Josephine's heavy lidded, soft black eyes. Most women found him irresistible.

Madame made him the incarnation of her prince and marshalled her spirits. When Louis Napoleon was arrested for poaching, she sent Nelson Chase to ask for the honor of representing him. When the verdict went against the prince, Madame paid his fine.

He was twenty-eight, Madame Sixty-one. But her inner infant cared nothing for age and probability. If it was not her destiny to sit on the throne of France, why had this princeling come?

In his unsupported exile, Louis Napoleon found it pleasant to talk to a woman who had known his Uncle Joseph and his grandfather Napoleon. Her talk of Paris amused him. It was the city of his most vivid imagination, and he had never been permitted to live there. He sometimes accepted Madame's hospitality; occasionally in the afternoon they played whist for money.

Eventually Madame arranged a dinner in his honor. Since this was only possible from her citadel, her Mansion, she moved her entourage to the Heights where she could confound the prince with her Bonaparte trophies and dazzle him with his grandmother's jewels. Cinderella's glass slipper was not more numenous than Madame's diamonds were to her.

Colonel Craft said, *"She made a supreme effort because she aimed for the throne of France."* It is impossible to know whether the Colonel's story is true or apocryphal or invented in the matrix of his contempt. *"On the day of the dinner,"* he said, *Madame Jumel chose to use a depilatory on her incipient mustache with such caustic effect, such inflammation and swelling, that she was unable to be present."*

Women, who can discuss most aspects of sexuality, will sometimes hesitate to use the word mustache in this context. If Madame could not be present at her banquet without revealing that she had had a mustache, her mortification was terrible.

Shortly after the miscarriage of the banquet in his honor, Louis Napoleon was alarmed by a letter from his mother. Although the Queen had made no reference to her illness, a friend had written, *"Revenez! Revenez!"* under her signature; and he understood that she was dying. Using the pseudonym Robinson, he slipped back to Switzerland to sit by her deathbed.

Madame's megalomania was not diminished. She insisted that the banquet table in her octagonal room, the room she had lined with mirrors, be left as it

150

had been set for the prince. Its ornaments: crystal, silver and ormolu, confections and fruit, were left as a monument to the prince who had seen them. So they remained for thirty years. The actors in Madame's dreams were interchangeable; and in time she came to think of it as the table she had set for Joseph, the King of Naples, the two Sicilies and Spain.

"*The King complimented me on the elegance of my table,*" she would say. "*It was worthy of a king and so I left it.*" She did, oblivious of the decaying food stuff, dust and spider webs; until her table became notorious in the city and her banquet the butt of knowing laughter.

With the setting of this table, Madame's self-imposed exile was over. She would leave her mansion to travel to Europe and summer in Saratoga but she would never lease it again.

23

"It is the image that binds us to our lost treasure, but it
is the loss that shapes the image."
Colette

Chase believed the air on the Heights was too
strong for Mary's lungs. Perhaps her malaise prevented
them from joining Madame immediately, and as long as
the Chases lived in Hoboken, Madame commuted
across the Hudson every Friday.

Still the Mansion's eighteen haunted rooms
needed human voices. Madame assumed the care of a
black family headed by Elizabeth Northrup whose
husband had been kidnapped and sold South into
slavery. Elizabeth had a daughter named Eliza, a four-
year-old like Madame's grandchild. Under the
circumstances, to give her child a home, Mrs. Northrup
was willing to work without wages. Madame, who had
been farmed out so often as a child, felt free to dispose
of Eliza Northrup as casually. That spring she sent
black Eliza to Hoboken as a playmate for Miss Eliza
Chase.

Black Eliza suffered. *"It was spring,"* she would
say. *"The birds and flowers were so gay and cheerful but I
was very sad being at the Chases."*

Madame had no friends in the usual sense.
Eleven servants whose testimony covered a great many
years, would swear that no lady ever called on Madame
Jumel. She sought the companionship of trades people
and they, as well as her servants, saw the gentler side of
her nature. Such friends made no demands and in their
company Madame escaped from the forces that drove

her dream of grandeur. She trusted working women as she could never trust a man, or any person she thought of as her social equal.

Charity Kennedy who owned a bakery in the City was part of Madame's surrogate family. It was Madame's habit to order pastry and to pick up Charity with it when she went to Hoboken. She talked to Charity, as she did to everyone, about the great men she had known; but she told Charity she had a son.

In the seemingly endless plateau of middle age, she was obsessed with the child she deserted. She told Charity she had married when she was very young and been forced to give her baby up. She said she heard from him often and at any time she might go to Providence and bring him home. Apparently she trusted Charity never to speak of her baby in front of Mary or Nelson Chase.

The story of the lost child would be repeated by servant after servant. Madame wanted to find her little boy and bring him home. Once she took Mary Steever with her to visit Ann Eliza Ballou and humbled herself to ask for news. Then she raged at Mary Steever for visiting Ann Eliza alone. Finally, perhaps because she didn't want an adolescent girl as her companion, she sent Mary back to her mother and adopted a boy.

"Is Jonny your own son?" asked David Carrol who was hired to mow her fields.

"No," Madame said. *"I got Jonny at the Refuge Asylum. I have a little boy, but I don't see him anymore."*

She told her seamstress about George Washington. *"I want him to come and live with me, but he is so well situated he can't do it."* She had learned as much from Ann Eliza.

Another servant thought she found a picture of

153

Madame's baby. *"I found a miniature picture, an oil painting of a little boy in Madame's drawer. I took it out to look at it, and when she saw me she told me to put it back. Later,"* said the same servant, *"Madame was showing me the boxwood border around the trees and my own little boy was along running in and out of the walk. He liked to step on the little branches that had split off and Madame told him to be careful. She said, 'Be a good boy and I will do for you as the world has done for my son I have but one child and that was a son'."*

She told Alonzo Northrup, who joined his mother in Madame's service, that there was a special room in the house where no one could sleep until her son came home.

When Mary was pregnant for the third time, the Chases joined Madame on the Heights. Then the house held four Elizas, two generations of Northrups and two generations of Jumels. Little Eliza Northrup, who was old enough to help in the house, remembered challenging her mistress. Madame had asked her to help set the table and she had refused.

"When I tell you to do something, you must mind me," Madame said, *"because you are my child."*

"I ain't your child."

"You are my child as much as Miss Eliza and you must mind me."

"You ain't my mother; my mother's a nigger."

The softness and sadness of Madame's answer startled Eliza. *"That's right. I never had but one child born to me and he was a son."*

Because Madame so often forgot the passage of time and spoke of Bowen as a little boy, her servants assumed he had died as a child and measuring Madame's guilt by her obsession, they assumed she had killed him. Obviously Madame couldn't have climbed in society with a bastard, and the half-suppressed stories of Stephen's death but she tried to stop speculation about her son. *"You must not believe what you hear,"* she said to Elizabeth Northrup. *"I did not kill my little boy at all. He is alive and will show up here some day."*

But Madame dreaded a confrontation with her son; and certainly she dreaded the reaction of Nelson Chase whose inheritance was threatened by a son, whose very existence violated the prenuptial agreement he had made with Madame. She was afraid of them both and endlessly postponed going to Providence.

Ironically, she never imagined the truth, that Bowen knew who she was. He watched her spectacular appearances in Saratoga for forty years and kept his secret better than she. He never mentioned their relationship, even to his wife.

Like his mother, who had taken the name Capet, George Washington Bowen mystified his birth. Many children imagine for a time that they are royal changelings trapped in an unworthy household. But Bowen never surrendered the fantasy. He believed his father had been the father of his country.

Before he died Reuben Ballou had given young George a pig skin pocketbook; four by five, with a strap and a hook, which he said, General Washington left with him. The money for his raising had been inside. George treasured the purse and passed it on to his oldest son as a wedding present.

The purse and the legend were cherished for generations. The family faith was re-enforced by Bowen's extraordinary resemblance to his alleged father. He had the same straight, prominent nose; heavy, overhung brow; high cheek bones; small, wide-set eyes and long, tight-set mouth. Like the General, he was a large man. As he grew older, he wore his hair as Washington had, and his resemblance to the great man grew ever more striking.

Ann Eliza said everyone in Providence knew George Washington was Bowen's father. But the Court called her wicked and depraved for suggesting that Washington might have committed adultery or visited a prostitute. She was advised to modify her story.

"The saying is every fool knows his mother," she said. *"But only a wise child knows his father."* (The Court was assured by then that none of Phebe's children knew their fathers). Ann Eliza tried to help Bowen further. *"Mother told me that some people in Rhode Island say that Uriah Bowne, the Mayor of Providence was Bowen's father. I always understood that when Mother spoke of General Washington as Bowen's father, she was joking. We always had a laugh about it...Mother said when Reuben Ballou was thrown from his horse, Washington came to see him several times. And Betsy Bowen lived there then, helping Mrs. Ballou with the work.*

Well, I've heard it said that Washington came through Providence several times during the Revolution. But I don't know from history in what year the Revolutionary War closed, or in what year General Washington resigned his commission in the Army. And I don't know in what year he was inaugurated as President. I think he served two terms but I really don't recollect. I only know that Major Ballou named the baby George Washington because he thought so much of him." Bowen's lawyer said it would help his case if the jury believed his father was Reuben Ballou, but Ann Eliza

156

wouldn't perjure herself.

There is no evidence that George Washington ever begot a child. Indeed it was common talk that if he could have fathered a son, he'd have made himself king. In any case, his last visit to Providence was in 1790 and Bowen was born four years later.

Bowen's face was dour, as if illegitimacy darkened his life. He was deeply ashamed of the circumstances of his birth, and rather than risk the epithet bastard, he told his wife he was an orphan. It was almost true. In spite of Freelove's devotion, no one had stood in loco parentis. Like his mother, he began working for victuals when he was six, and still he lived the American dream. He was a self-made man and his home on a high street in Providence looked down on the low street of his birth. In terse, almost biblical terms, he outlined his life for the Court.

"I was somewhere in the neighborhood of six when Major Ballou died. He treated me like a son and he would call me sonny or George and tell me to go to the slaughter house and fetch something. I accompanied him when he carried meat in a wagon once or twice a week. And I saw him make entries in a book when he sold meat after I became so I knew what handwriting was. I didn't learn to read writing the first time I went to school - I didn't learn.

When Major Ballou died, then I worked in the neighborhood of a year with William Ballou, the son of the butcher and he was a butcher in the same business as his father. I lived in the house with his family and he was married, and I worked in the slaughter house with him. He agreed to pay me wages, but he didn't. I never got any.

When I was nine or ten, I was put out in the country to live in Smithfield with the Mowrys. They were farmers and lived twelve miles out. And I worked for him for a spell and at other places on the same terms - for victuals. And I stayed a spell and then was transferred into Cumberland along with Joseph Jenks, a farmer. Then I came back to Providence and went to live with Mr. Weeden to learn baking. I was between fourteen and fifteen, it might be. I was young and Daniel Hull was in apprentice working with him too, and we would talk, same as any apprentice. I didn't go to school. Mr. Weeden's life was so he couldn't let me go. I was there three years or so, but not after.

I considered myself a man when I was fourteen. I was big enough to take care of myself and I came to the City. There's about twenty folks on a packet boat. I didn't come alone. I came to the City for ten or fifteen years to buy things and for pleasure. I used to put up at Lavinia's house down in the City. I took a meal and tea and lodging and breakfast with them too.

Then I was a clerk and then I was employed in weaving until peace was proclaimed in 1815 when I was twenty-one, and I knew my wife ten years before I married her. She was eight or nine in the beginning and her parents were dead. She lived with her brother, Benjamin Westcott, about a ten minute walk from the Ballou's The distance, I could not name it.

Then I went to Asa Newell, in his store. Next I bought out Major Thayer and went into the grocery by myself and continued in it for several years. Then into the India Rubber business. Then into lottery business until they broke it up. It is not legal now, but it was legal then. Since then I went into the grocery and then I gave it up to my son.

The first I saw Madame Jumel", he said in answer to a question, *"she was going into the United States Hotel*

158

in Saratoga in the State of New York. All the folks around there said. 'There goes Madame Jumel.' And I saw her walking on the walks at the Hotel or riding in her carriage in parts of the City or up on the piazza. My wife said, 'She's a fine looking woman.' And I said, 'Well, she is.' And I never spoke to her. And I never said anything to my wife about my relationship with Madame Jumel. Because I was married proper. And I didn't know a bastard could inherit. "

Mary bore a son, William Ingles Chase, but this child comforted no one. Mary's strength never returned. Chase blamed the air on the Heights, but tuberculosis had smoldered in Mary since childhood. Its eruption in middle age followed a familiar pattern. With or without the attendance of a doctor, its course was inevitable: lassitude, exhaustion, loss of weight, the pallor of anemia, the flush of fever, loss of circulation, coughing, and hemorrhages which filled the lungs with blood. The fragile heroines of the age, Camille, Violetta, Mimi, Heathcliff's Cathy...wasted as Mary did, with time for long thoughts and last farewells.

Mary had found no way to resist the suction of her being into Madame's She never released herself from the childish conviction that her all-powerful stepmother was always right. As she surrendered her body, first to pregnancy, then to death, she withdrew what affection she felt for Nelson Chase; he was only another child in her mother's keep. Gratefully she entered the helplessness which bound her to Madame. *"Bring up and educate my children, "* she said. *"If you see to them, I can die happy. "* With these words she departed the life she had never lived.

Madame's grief was inconsolable. *"My dear little*

angel, my angel Mary." She lay in bed for ten days.

"Then," said Nelson Chase, *"Madame Jumel took my daughter and had charge of her and assumed control. After a little she also had control of my son...And she had control of them and kept them both."*

24

:"Who can refute a sneer?"
William Paley

Madame's legal matters; deeds, indentures and foreclosures, were handled by Nelson Chase, who acting as house-lawyer, remained in a filial relationship, bound by his weakness to Madame's strength. He had followed his mother-in-law from Greenwich Street to Chambers Street, to the Heights, to Hoboken to Grande Street and back to the Heights. Now he went with her to Saratoga. *"I always went with her,"* he said. *"For the support of the family was borne by Madame Jumel."*

Madame first visited Saratoga in 1819, when Stephen was in France, Mary ailing, and both women excluded from the homes of their neighbors. Now she shrewdly invested in land; she was as acute as ever in matters of finance. She bought one parcel of fifty acres from which she leased twenty-seven lots; and a farm of one hundred acres of which she leased thirty-two. In time she would own the Adelphi and Rip Van Dam hotels, all the land bordering Lake Avenue, as well as the land which would encompass Saratoga's famous race track.

She called Saratoga her 'retreat' and she returned there when life in New York was not rewarding. Saratoga had no rigid class distinctions. Madame and her wards were accepted, at least at first, at face value.

Society visited the Springs in the dog days of August. Young women, widows and adventurers came

161

to meet gentlemen, millionaires and politicians. Senators and presidents filled the hotel living rooms with smoke from their cigars: Marten Van Buren, Henry Clay, Andrew Jackson, Daniel Webster, Calhoun, Buchanan, Tyler and Filmore... Hundreds of a simple people like Bowen and his wife came to pretend for a fortnight that they were part of that great society their positions at home denied them.

"Why do they come here? Why do they wish to mingle with a crowd of queer strangers and drag out these tiresome days of artificial entertainment?" asked the mayor of New York, who came himself for twenty years.

In the beginning, they came for the waters, which collecting minerals from faults in the earth, emerge in many springs; always effervescent, sometimes salty, sometimes tasting of bicarbonate of soda, sometimes of sulfur and rotten eggs. The waters were (indeed, are) thought to have miraculous powers of a general nature. Like the waters of Lourdes, the waters of Saratoga may be taken internally or externally either as prevention or cure.

It was fashion, rather than the waters, that attracted Bowen and his mother. The great hotels were her natural milieu. In their parlors and on their piazzas, gesture was everything. Obeisance was paid to ostentation: the largest tip, the longest cigar butt burning in an ashtray, the fastest carriage, the most extravagant wardrobe, were honored. On the piazzas diamonds were appraised like decorations for valor.

But even in the best hotels, days dragged. The United States the Grand Union, and the Congress were as big as streetcar barns. The United States, where Madame stayed, could seat a thousand persons in its

162

dining room, but the food was bad and the service less indulgent than an Army mess. Breakfast took twenty minutes; dinner twenty-five; supper twenty. Gongs rang at seven-thirty and again at seven-thirty two. At the signal, a double row of waiters marched to the kitchen and returned with a course of food. Again, at the sound of a the gong, they removed plates and marched back to the kitchen. Other rooms were no more comfortable. The white washed bedrooms where Madame and her family used to stay were furnished with bed, bureau, chair and commode. The parlor was known as the largest, most sparsely furnished room in the world. Islands of wicker chairs, wide to accommodate hoop skirts, were set in groves of ferns and potted palms where cliques met to stake out their claims and exchange gossip.

The heart of the hotel was external. The piazza's half mile of rocking chairs was both theater and promenade, as actors and audience rocked and strolled as they studied one another. On the piazza of the United States, Joseph Bonaparte, grown monstrously fat, learned that Napoleon was dead.

They say Madame was part of the reception committee that welcomed Joseph. They say she was at the banquet when he almost died, clutching his throat, struggling to say chat; because the kitchen calico was hidden in the room and he was allergic. Legend says that Madame was permitted by the meretricious widows of Doctor Rush and Governor Clinton to join the circle which formed around the Marquis de Lafayette because *"in spite of her criminal intimacy with Burr, which brought her dismissal from the ranks of Diana, Lafayette had known Colonel Burr during the Revolution."* Madame was in Paris when Lafayette was

163

in Saratoga, but such stories attached themselves like barnacles to her name.

The invention and spreading of rumor were the business of the piazzas. Those rivals for attention, Mrs. De Witt Clinton and Madame Stephen Jumel were obvious subjects. Mrs. Clinton was the mentor of virtue, but Madame with her aura of sin had the greater following. Bowen was not alone, watching her entrances and exits. The groundlings loved to see her take her place in the three o'clock parade of carriages which raced down Broadway, out Union Avenue, to the Lake and back. It was Madame's joy to be first.

There were other heroines. Both natives and summer people doted on the witch, Angela Tubbs, who when she was fifteen, had loved a soldier in the army of General Burgoyne. When Burgoyne was defeated, the people of Saratoga hung the child on a gallows all day without letting her die. When they let her go, Angela severed her connection with humanity. For the next ninety years she lived in the woods. Trappers sometimes saw her leaping from ledge to ledge, strong and erect even in her great old age. They said they saw her raising her arms and calling to the wind and rain, thunder and lightning, as if those wild elements were congenial. Sometimes she roamed the streets of Saratoga, always wrapped in the same plaid blanket; and even when she was very old, one hundred and four, toothless and unkempt, her eyes blazed with a power and intelligence that made reasonable men get out of her way.

Saratoga loved to associate Madame with the witch. One evening at a revival meeting, someone called out. *"Pray for Angela Tubbs and Madame Jumel."* Madame stumbled from the tent.

164

When she saw she was mocked in the great hotels, she withdrew. As she said, *"Without giving the matter more than ten minutes consideration,"* she added the Hodgeman Cottage to her holdings and made it her summer residence.

The Hodgeman-Jumel cottage is a pleasant Greek Revival building, a temple with pillars and pediments, back and front. A piazza, backed by French doors opened into her music room. But the house was as divided as Madame herself. The gracious, high ceilinged upper rooms rest on a windowless basement - lined with the cells where Madame's unpaid servants slept.

Perhaps Madame's impulsive purchase was inspired by the geography of Providence and her first perception of respectability. Her Cottage is in the upper town and from its eminence she could look down on the mansard roofs of the great hotels, on the wine glass elms of Broadway and the temple springs of Congress Park. With characteristic conceit, she called her relatively modest house, the Tuileries.

Rocking there on her own piazza, she gathered a coterie of young ladies and, like an old veteran, doled out the story of her life to anyone who would listen. Many an adolescent girl was forbidden to approach that wicked piazza but, like her servants and the trades people who served as companions, the young people were not critical, and Madame bound them to her with what wiles she possessed.

At seventy-eight, she lived in a state of promise, still looking forward to the adventure that would make her immortal. It was an age of Pride, when the desire for esteem in the eyes of others was considered noble. Racine, La Rochefoucauld, Milton, Voltaire, Hume,

Kant, Stendhal and Balzac all spoke of pride as the engine of culture and source of civilization. But only the French combined pride and the longing for fame in one word, la gloire. The concept was masculine, but the masculine side of Madame's nature had long been dominant. She hungered for la gloire as Burr and Hamilton had; for la gloire as personified by the Emperor Napoleon.

Madame returned to France. This time her companion was sixteen-year-old Eliza Chase. Such was Madame's vitality, that Eliza passed as her niece, as if they were separated by one, rather than two generations. The old woman called herself Madame Burr. Neither Burr's name nor his rank were useful to her in the United States. But such was the psychic distance between Europe and America, that although Burr had not held office for fifty years, she could present herself there as wife of the Vice President of the United States. Sometimes, without a trace of irony, she called herself the Vice Queen, as if the United States were a monarchy and she the wife of the Viceroy, one who rules in the King's absence.

She arrived in Paris as the curtain rose on the Second Empire. The city was as ambiguous as the title Madame chose for herself. Opposites coexisted and the tension between the masquerade and reality vibrated. On the surface life was vulgar and alluring: a spectacle with red velvet and gold leaf, eagles and trumpets, black lace and diamonds, the clatter of carriages on cobblestones and the ring of iron horse shoes. Behind the graceful facades of the great boulevards, was a shadow world of poverty and crime; labyrinths where ten-year-old prostitutes, beggars, thieves, pimps, and murderers, hid in vermin infested rooms - an apt reflection of Madame's autumnal self, her persona and her secrets.

The House of Worth on the Rue de la Paix provided costumes for courtesans and women of the court. No excess was too great. Velvet and satin brocade were re-embroidered with colored silks or gold and silver thread, or all three. Gowns were finished with yards of lace, tassels, fringes, feathers, ribbons and flowers; and skirts were draped over telescoping crinoline cages.

It was said that as a woman rose in rank, her bodice fell proportionately. Madame would not bare her old flesh, but she shopped at the House of Worth and soon wrote, asking Nelson Chase to deposit more money to her account.

25

"The ordinary life of men is like that of the saints.
They all seek their satisfaction, and differ only in the
object in which they place it."
Pascal

The Princeling Madame had known in
Hoboken, in a final coup, restored the Empire and
reigned as Napoleon III. His first concern was to
establish a court. His nobility had to be housed. In the
Revolution of '48, the Tuileries had been gutted.
Napoleon III had the palace divided like the pigeon
holes of a desk, into narrow, often windowless
apartments. That spring two reception halls had been
restored and the Imperial fete began.

The Count and Countess de la Pagerie invited
Madame and Eliza to the first ball. The son of
Madame's old friend, the Countess who lived with her
thirty-five years before, Henri Tasher, was still grateful
for Madame's courtesy to his mother. He was the
Emperor's Grand Master of Ceremonies and it was his
function to arrange the balls, banquets, masquerades
and fetes champetre so dear to courtiers and aspirants
like Madame Jumel.

Not everyone was awed. *"Four things matter at
the Tuileries:"* Jules de Goncourt wrote, *"youth, beauty,
diamonds and a dress."* Madame had diamonds and a
dress. As she climbed the marble stairs to the Gallery
of Diane, she saw herself reflected, as every woman did,
in the gold breast plates of the Cent Garde. Seeing
youth and beauty in those distorting mirrors she took
them for her own.

This account is from the journal of one of the young ladies who sat at Madame's feet listening to her tales of la gloire. With Madame's words echoing in her mind, she wrote in the first person quoting.

"*My toilette was magnificent. I was one blaze of diamonds. And as I entered with my party of ladies, people whispered, 'Here comes the Vice Queen of America and she has come this night to stab Louis Napoleon. Beware!'*

When I heard this, I tossed my head and sat down surrounded by my train. Finally I thought I would speak to the Emperor. He had been dancing with his cousin Matilde and was resting. So I rose to my feet - on a lower step sat Jerome Bonaparte - and I waved my hand saying 'Make way for the Vice Queen.' And he rose very haughtily and looked at me.

I passed on with my train and stood before Louis Napoleon, and stamping my foot, I said 'Sire! Sire!' I stamped my foot again - the court behind me with outstretched arms to seize the dagger they thought I carried - 'I have come to present... to present...' I bowed low. The court behind me made another step in advance. 'To present myself, Sire...' Then a very low bow. 'I am the widow of Colonel Burr, the ex-Vice President of the United States. I am Madame Jumel from Fort Washington.'

'Ah, my dear Madame Jumel,' said the Emperor. 'My dear Madame Jumel, I am so glad to see you. When did you leave Fort Washington?'

We conversed a great while together about my place and how I beat him at whist and so on. But I did not ask him for the money he owed me - the three hundred dollars."

Madame's tale is a transparent melodrama. But

169

it is more accurate than the Parisian newspaper which assumed a friendship between Burr and Louis Napoleon. Madame was a femme sole only in matters of finance; in society she would always be the wife of her husband. *"In the first Parisian ball,"* reported la Patrie, *"the brilliant toilette of a stranger wearing an incredible amount of diamonds attracted the attention of all present. In a moment attention turned to intense curiosity, for Louis Napoleon was observed to accost the lady and to remain some moments in conversation with her. The enigma was soon solved. The lady was the widow of Aaron Burr, formerly Vice President of the United States, with whom Louis Napoleon had been on terms of intimacy in that country. And at the end of fifteen years, the Emperor recognized the widow of his old friend."*

On the twelfth of May, Louis Napoleon symbolically restored the Empire by presenting the officers of the Army with banners bearing the Imperial eagle. Henri Tasher arranged for Madame to be present. In her vanity she saw the ceremony as a vindication of her boldness, a measure of her loyalty to the Bonaparte cause. She had been arrested in 1815 for flaunting such an emblem. For Madame it was epiphany, and her former shame became a source of exquisite pride. *"My dear father,"* Eliza wrote to Nelson Chase, *"We were detained longer than we expected in order to attend the ceremony of presenting the eagle to the army on the Champs de Mars."* In spite of Eliza's terseness, the drama of the returned eagles impressed her as it did her great aunt.

Madame sat for her portrait and had lithographs made for reproduction. Her decolletage was modest, but age enforced no other sanction. In the Biblioteque

Nationale that lithograph is listed as Madame Burr, Widow of the late Aaron Burr, Vice President of the United States, formerly Madame Jumel, heroine of New York.

In that same mood of exhilaration she had liveries made for three postilions, in the sour green Josephine had loved. And she bought garters, or had them made, with mottos in gold embroidery summoning up the wistful story of her life - *Gloria* on one leg, *y Amour* on the other.

Finally on the road to Bordeaux, finding the way blocked by a company of soldiers, she rose in her seat and shouted, *"Make way for the Vice Queen of America!"* And the poilus fell back in the hedgerows.

Crossing the Atlantic Madame's royal persona suffered a sea change. It was hard to maintain a French image in Harlem Heights, but she did not surrender it easily. Once in residence she notified the little town of Carmensville on the Hudson that on a certain day, at a certain hour, she would drive down the main street to show them her postilions in their new livery. They pelted her carriage with stones and eggs.

She resumed target practice. *"Mr. Bailey,"* she said one day to a workman, *"Do you see that bird over there? I could take his head off with my first shot."*

While her spirits were still buoyant, she made a pilgrimage to Saratoga, where postilions and livery were honored. There, in her fashion, she reproduced the drama of the presentation of the eagles to the Army on the Champ de Mars. Madame had a banner made of white satin with a gold fringe and an appliqued and embroidered figure of Liberty grasping a pike crowned with a liberty cap. Like the eagle on Madame's yellow calash, the eagle on the finial of the staff was decked

171

with laurel.   Assuming for the moment, the role of Napoleon III, Madame presented the banner to the Citizen's Corps of Utica.   The ceremony had been rehearsed;   and the corps commander accepted the gift *"with eloquent words in her praise."*

That evening she entertained the officers of the Corps at the Tuileries.   Those young men, who had never been to France, who revered Napoleon as a demigod, listened to stories of the Emperors Madame had known with appropriate awe.   That night the Corps sang the lullabies of la gloire, the <u>Marseillaise</u> and <u>America,</u> under her window.   An obsequious letter from the Citizens of Utica took its framed place in the memorial hall of her Mansion.

26

"Riches attract the attention, the consideration and
congratulations of Mankind."
John Adams

In the fall of the following year, in 1853,
Madame crossed the Atlantic for the last time; taking
both children, twelve-year-old Willy and eighteen-year-
old Eliza. She wanted to inspect her holdings in Malta,
to consider investments in Sicily, and most urgently to
arrange a marriage for her grand niece. Eliza Chase,
looking to unmarketable spinsterhood, felt the pressure
of time as keenly as Madame.

Like her mother, she was plump and bovine.
No poudre de riz, no restricting corset could make her
seem fragile or confer on her *"that delicate beauty which
no healthful comeliness can ever bestow."* But what she
lacked in charm, Madame could match in financial
endowment. She would make the most of Eliza's
assets: her sheltered life, her passivity, her lack of
passion and humor. These qualities were much
admired.

To this end, Nelson Chase invested Madame
with his power of attorney, giving her authority to
arrange a match between his daughter and Paul
Raymond Guilliam Pery of Bordeaux, whom neither
he nor his daughter had ever met.

Madame had no folie de doubt. She had known
the Perys as friends of Stephen. Her dead angel had
gone to Mlle. Laurau's with Trissier Pery. Paul
Raymond's father was neither rich nor prominent. He
was a notaire - less than a lawyer, more than a notary,

but rich men are not often for sale. Paul and Eliza met for the first time in December.

Madame established a base for herself and her charges at the Hotel de France, and every afternoon for a fortnight they met in the home of Paul's parents. *"I saw them every day as near as I can recollect,"* Paul would tell the court. He, too, was promised a share of Madame's estate and he, too, would have to defend his inheritance. *"I never saw my present wife alone. Always in the company of Madame Jumel and my brother-in-law, Nelson Chase."*

"Had you any affection for that girl?" asked Bowen's lawyer, hoping to elicit Pery's unworthiness as Madame's heir.

"Yes, Sir," said Pery.

"Was it strong or otherwise?

"Well, that's a curious question. I may say strong."

Madame accomplished all she thought seemly in the two weeks because the interval between marriage and courtship was appropriate, she trusted absence would make Paul and Eliza no less fond, sent Chase home and continued her journey. It was part of her intention to make this, her farewell to Europe, the climax of the Chase children's education. They spent several weeks in Rome where Madame had arranged to sit with her wards for the artist, Alcide Ercole. He was a painter of facile but mediocre talent who had been elected to the British Royal Academy for his flattering portraits of fashionable women.

He painted the old courtesan as she saw herself then, Mater Dolorosa, with tender smile and tragic eyes. She is seated on a dais on a red velvet throne with Willy and Eliza on either side on the level below. To wholly establish her dominance, the young people are dwarfed. Willy gazes up at his great aunt, and Eliza bends her matronly body toward her. In fashionable portraits there are conventional compliments. Ercole knew them all. Madame's hands are as youthful as Eliza's, her hair as rich in henna lights, and the curve of her bosom is more graceful. A lace mantilla frames her old face, drawing all lines up to her magnificent eyes. The vee of her grackle green gown balances the width of her side curls; and a lace shawl, a work of great beauty, falls under one arm and over the other, suggesting suppleness and vitality. Ercole painted the falling flesh of Madame's cheek and the folds under her eyes, but her nose is as pert, her mouth as sweet and her eyes as remarkable as when she sat for St. Memin fifty-seven years before.

From Rome the little entourage moved on to Naples. No Victorian tourist failed to visit Pompeii and Herculaneum, to swoon at the sublime evidence of nature's caprice and man's mortality. From Naples they sailed to Malta.

The nature of Madame's business there is unknown. Visitors like herself lived in charming villas with tiled patios where carefully nurtured lemon trees bore fruit as large as oranges and carefully nurtured orange trees bore bitter oranges with blood-red flesh. But the island was at the mercy of erratic winds; and fogs which restricted the harbor for weeks on end depressed and enervated European visitors. Madame and the Chase children moved on to Sicily.

Chase had armed her with several documents. In addition to his power of attorney, she carried a draft in her favor for 15,000 francs and a letter of introduction to Ciamonte, Duke of Palermo: *"Sire: My son and daughter will be traveling with Madame Burr*

175

and Madame will visit Palermo after inspecting her holdings in Malta..."

No people on earth were more insistent on female virtue than those Sicilians, who from the beginning of history had seen their women raped by invaders. Madame was a chaperon of Sicilian scrupulosity. But at seventy-nine she had an amorous adventure which sent her reeling back to Paris. A prince pursued her.

She fled in May, when the African heat of a Sicilian summer is insufferable to northerners; but the climate of Sicily is not part of Madame's fantasy. As always that dream involved a prince whose courtship became boring as his love became carnal.

"I went to the palace of the Duke," she told one of her young ladies, *"and the great hall opens upon seven halls lined with mirrors. And when I saw this hall, I stamped my foot and said, 'This place shall be mine.' I did not know the Duke was a widower, but the woman must have reported my speech to her master, for the next day, the Duke alighted at my lodgings all arrayed in laces and diamonds. And as he stepped from his carriage, a friend asked him where he was going and what presentation was to take place. And he said, 'I am going to present myself to the Vice Queen of America.'*

We conversed in French and, when he took leave of me, he kissed my hand six times. But when he was done, I said to Eliza, 'That man is going to bore us. Let's leave for Paris tonight.'

And no sooner were we in Paris when a beautiful letter came in French from the Duke, offering his hand and half of what he possessed if only I would marry him. I did not answer his letter and soon he made his appearance and implored me to marry him. 'But,' I said, 'I am faithful to

176

the memory of Colonel Burr. *I bear you the celestial affection angels in Heaven bear one another. I love you like a brother.' And he kissed my hand many times and departed, overcome with grief."*

Madame had a serious match to consider. In Paris, she began negotiations with M. Jean Pery.

"Paris. May 22, 1854.

Sir: I am in no wise offended by the questions you address me within your letter of the 20th instance, and I answer with the greatest pleasure because their object is the happiness of my niece, upon whom rests all my affections, as the greater part of my fortune is destined for her and her brother.

That fortune may be estimated at two million dollars. In any case, if my niece would marry your son, I would secure her an income of five thousand francs. Once married, if my niece, as I hope, be happy in her household and be to me what she has always been, my intention is to advance her beyond the share which is coming to her and which I destine to from this day.

Such, Sir, are my intentions with respect to my fortune. With that, independently of what you do for them, the young people will be comfortable. If these prospects are realized, I have no doubt, Sir, but that my niece would receive among you a welcome and attachment equal to that which her family has for her, and that her presence would increase the joys of the new family which hereafter would be hers.

If the position which I offer my niece is agreeable to you, I do not doubt, Sir, that the conclusion be favorable to your son.

I shall replay upon the details which you will give me of your situation in case you wish that the affair should take place.

Pray, Sir, receive the homage of my perfect consideration,
Eliza Burr"

Pery believed he could extort further consideration from Madame. She answered with clarity.

"Sir: Your letter of this morning informs me fully of your intentions with regard to the dower you suggest for the wife your son has chosen. I understand all your solicitude as a father. But I guarantee the sum of 5,000 francs. By all the contracts which you may require, I guarantee that sum. Moreover, my niece lost her mother in infancy and it is I who have brought her up. She never left me and I have a true affection for her. Without setting today the share she may have in my estate, that share may be considerable and my testamentary disposition, that share will be assured her. Accept, Sir, my very sincere salutations.
Eliza Burr"

The elder Pery conceded and sent his son to Paris to continue his courtship. The indifference of the young people and the paucity of their acquaintance would startle the court which appraised their right to Madame's money. Bowen's lawyer elicited the coldness of their engagement.

"I saw my present wife in the latter part of May, 1854, when I met them in Paris," young Pery said.

"And how much were you in their company?" asked Chauncey Shaffer.

"I dined with them every day."

"Would you have married your wife without money?"

"Most undoubtedly."

"You would?"

"Yes, Sir."

"You have been asked if you would have married your wife if she had had no money. Would you have married her without your father and mother's consent?"

"I would not have done so without my father's consent."

Eliza was cross-examined too. *"Did the letters Madame Jumel wrote M. Pery influence you?"*

"It did, to marry, Sir."

"You were about eighteen years of age?"

"Yes."

"Did you understand the pecuniary situation of M. Pery Sr.?"

"I understood that he was a man of means and respectability."

"Did you have affection for his son?"

"At what time do you mean?"

"At the time Madame Jumel wrote those letters."

"I can't say I had any great affection. I wish to explain. It is what the French call marriage de convenience, for parents have more to do with it than anyone else. I left it all to my aunt."

"Were you willing to marry anyone she thought fit and proper?"

"No, Sir. Not anyone."

"When you did marry him, had you come to the conclusion that you would marry him without regard for money?"

"No, Sir, I had not."

"Did you expect money from his father?"

No, Sir, I expected a settlement from my aunt."

"One hundred thousand francs dot. $20,000

in gold."

    "You received twenty thousand dollars in gold?"
No, Sir. I mean five thousand francs."
"Is that what influenced you as money in hand?"
"Yes, Sir. She gave me the money."
"Every year?"
"Yes, Sir."
"Did you receive more than five thousand francs?"
"I expect I received more."

Perhaps the twenty thousand dollars so ambiguously referred to and so carelessly pursued by Bowen's lawyer was neither dot nor negotiable, but the price of Madame's freedom from her niece.

On the fifteenth of July, the young couple were married in a civil ceremony by the Mayor of Bordeaux, and on the following day, the ceremony was repeated in both the Catholic and Episcopal churches in Bordeaux. In both cases the United States Consul gave Eliza away. Madame, assured that the Perys would be united in the eyes of the United States, France and God, sailed on the tenth. *"My aunt got sick before my marriage,"* said Eliza Pery without elaboration.

27

"And I have seen the Eternal footman hold my coat
and snicker."
T. S. Eliot

Nelson Chase described the Mansion as it was
then, when he and his son Willy lived there alone with
Madame and her servants. *"The homestead was kept as a
country seat,"* he said, *"much of it in a state of wild
nature. There was pasture land, meadow land, and an
occasional patch of corn or potatoes - gardens where
vegetables were raised. But a large part of the estate was
wooded and the wood was cut for fuel for the family."*
Chase took no pleasure in the management of his
mother-in-law's manor, and in Madame's long
absences, it was much abused by her neighbors.

When Stephen was alive, they stole his grapes.
Now they grazed Madame's pastures, stripped her
gardens and fruit trees; and her forty acre wood lot was
a public source of timber as well as firewood.

Madame defended her land with all the
resources of her waning power. She supervised
everything, even the slaughter of pigs. She threatened
to bring law suits and practiced with her pistols. Once
she threatened to shoot a hired man for not pursuing
real or imagined thieves. She fenced ninety-four acres;
but her fences were honored only in the breach. When
scows on the Harlem River began carrying her lumber
to sell in the City, she asked for police protection. The
City sent two men. To ensure the only loyalty she
thought she could command, she paid them as if they
were in her hire. They resented her feudal manner and

for a bottle of whiskey helped her neighbors cut wood. *"Oh Alonzo,"* Madame said, *"if my son were here, you can be sure that he would find the thieves."*

Madame's longing for her son was renewed by the death of Lavinia Ballou. The circumstances shocked and saddened her. As Ann Eliza told the Court, *"Mother was confined to her bed two days and the second night she got up and hung herself with the cord of the window sash. The afternoon before, the doctor said she was stricken with death. And he said she had been dead twenty minutes before we cut her down. And it was the agony of death that gave her the strength to get up."*

Then Madame tried to renew her friendship with Ann Eliza but Ann Eliza, who had shared Lavinia's long knowledge and ancient grudge, could not forgive. Madame, wholly bereft of caring family, cut Ann Eliza and her children from her will.

The old woman improved her property. She had a well blasted in the yard, and inspired by the upturned earth, told the well diggers to look for buried treasure; treasure buried by Captain Kidd or fleeing Tories. They would testify that she was mad. She installed gas lights and a bathroom. She desecrated the Mansion's lovely rooms with Aubusson carpets, horsehair upholstery, little tables with bowed legs, whatnots covered with bibelots, dark bitumen paintings in scroll saw frames. She littered the rooms with fashionable clutter: bull rushes in alabaster vases, cupids suspended on invisible wires, easel paintings, figurines...In the parlor she had a dais built to hold a red velvet arm chair so that she could preside as she had in Ercole's portrait.

No fashion induced Madame to alter the banquet table in the octagonal room which remained as it had been set for Louis Napoleon. It startled Alonzo when he joined his mother in Madame's service. *"It was all set out,"* he said, *"with wine glasses and all and punch. I looked at it hard the first time, but I soon became accustomed."* Those who knew Madame doted on her folly. Visitors came specifically to gape. Dickens, who visited New York in 1848, either saw Madame's table or was told about it; for he attributed a similar table to the mad recluse, Miss Havisham, in *Great Expectations.*

Except as she befriended people in her hire, Madame was as reclusive as Miss Havisham. Mr. Bailey, the plumber, was sometimes the butt of her niggardly whims. He called to collect a dollar and fifty cents: *"But I have no such sum in the house, Mr. Bailey."* Then, waiting until he had opened the door to tease him, *"Mr. Bailey, if you'll drop the fifty cents, I'll give you a dollar..."*

"Mr. Bailey," she called to him once from a window as he approached, *"you must wait until I am ready to receive you in the French style. Stay where you are until I call you."* He waited.

"Now, Mr. Bailey, you may approach the door and tap gently on the knocker three times. My valet will open the door and address you in French."

"I don't understand French, Madame."

"Do as I say."

Mr. Bailey knocked three times and John the coachman opened the door wearing a red fez, with a chintz wrapper tied around his waist. *"I'll bang your jaw,"* he said.

Madame appeared. *"John,"* she said, *"you mustn't bang Mr. Bailey's jaw. You should have said bon jour."*

She swung like a pendulum between avarice and generosity. When an engineer from the City called to tell her their fence was on her side of the property line and that they would correct the boundary; she gave the gentleman lunch and when they had finished insisted that he accept a check for five hundred dollars.

Madame enjoyed the patience of Inspector Speers more than any other caller. She kept him in the front hall for hours, regaling him with the stories she had perfected on the young women of Saratoga: extracting from him an occasional "Yes, Madame" or "Really, Madame!" When his attention wandered, she invented new wonders. She claimed the friendship of Talleyrand, Charles X and Louis Philippe. She showed him the room where Lafayette slept. She invented a story about her cypress trees, saying Napoleon, who had them from the Khedive of Egypt, had given them to Mr. Jumel. Burr's simple story of the visit of two sachems from the Cayuga nation became a council of war. And the dinner Washington gave for his cabinet was extended in time, so that it still included every President of the United States.

As Madame's sense of being wronged by life became acute, she sued society at large. She sued for Burr's pension as Colonel back to his retirement in 1788. The Veteran's Bureau responded with embarrassment and concern - until they investigated and their letters became stern.

"Madame: The question of divorce must be met. You state to me the matter was dropped, but I am asked to produce the record." The correspondence continued until, like Phebe's suit against her landlord, it was abated by the death of the plaintiff.

Madame won a suit brought by Catherine Jumel Ohignon of Bordeaux, who challenged Madame's right

184

to Stephen's estate; claiming that Madame Jumel had chosen not to live with her husband and had been estranged from him at the time of his death. Madame proved she had always been as she signed herself, Stephen's "loving and faithful wife."

She sued for her interest in Jumel's office at 57 Pearl Street, purchased by him in 1811 and sold by Madame's attorney in 1829, demanding one third of the building's worth and one third of the rent collected since Stephen's death.

She successfully sued for the price of the chalice, ciborium, ostensoire, and vestments which Stephen had given to the old Cathedral of St. Patrick's. In all innocence, the Bishop of Boston wrote on her behalf: *"It is certainly time that the matter should be attended to, at least now, after thirty years. Madame Jumel is a widow now and it appears that she stands greatly in need of money. Surely, under the circumstances, not a moment's further delay ought to be suffered. Especially since it is well ascertained that the debt is a just one and should be paid...Now, Right Reverend Sir, will you have the kindness to let the trustees of the Cathedral know how this matter stands in order that a speedy settlement may be made."*

Madame no longer trusted Nelson Chase: and in spite of the fact that he had been Burr's advocate in the divorce proceedings, she hired Charles O'Conor to act in her behalf. He was at her service until in July 1851, at Chase's suggestion, he drew up a will for her signature. The testament was reasonable and probably close to Madame's intent. The bulk of her estate was divided between the Perys and the Chases; Stephen's niece was remembered; the servants were rewarded and charities acknowledged with token bequests. But

185

Madame bitterly resented the preemption of her sense of time, the anticipation of her death; and perhaps, most deeply, the usurpation of the power with which she controlled them all. She dismissed O'Conor for conspiring with Nelson Chase, and turned again to Thomas Connolly, the man who had defended her against the charge of murdering Stephen.

In her eighty-second year, in a burst of paranoia and energy, Madame recruited a legion to protect her estate from plunder and her person from assassination. Twenty indigent Frenchmen answered her call to arms - but except for the sentries at her gates, they were given sticks instead of guns. No one, however, lacked a uniform. Madame improvised costumes as bizarre as John's French livery. Willy, who was commissioned as a Commander in Madame's army, wore his costume proudly. But Nelson Chase would deny that he ever wore what he called his "extraordinary uniform."

To the delight of small boys, Madame drilled her troops personally. Boys watched her from many vantages. She and her army could be seen from the foot bridge over the swamp, which children on the Heights crossed on their way to school; from the tops of the Broadhurst family mausoleums; from the old deserted house at 155th Street and Eighth Avenue; from the opposite shore of the Harlem River and from the river itself.

Every morning at ten o'clock Madame appeared, thin and erect on her old gray horse. She led her parcel of men along the bluff of the River, along Edgecomb Avenue, up 159th Street - around and around the boundaries of her estate until she drew them up at parade rest and dismissed them. Occasionally boys in rowboats and rafts on the river aligned their vessels in a kind of naval salute. Madame would pull up her horse and stare at them sternly, never really knowing whether they mocked or applauded.

Every evening Sergeant Wasserman, standing under the portico of the house sounded taps on his bugle for the benefit of the men in the barn. She slept badly. It was her habit to rouse the household with alarms, to wake her soldiers to repel real or imagined brigands.

Sometimes she went abroad in her carriage. A member of that society which had repelled Madame Jumel, remembered seeing her as a child. *"My father and I,"* wrote Mrs. John King Renaselaer, *"passed an old black barouche, long since passed from fashion, and through the windows of that quaint black carriage, a shriveled face framed in a great black bonnet looked out at me. There was something about that strange countenance that made me turn to my father and ask excitedly who it was. He hemmed and hawed, as if unwilling to pass such knowledge on to a child. Then he said 'That's Madame Jumel, for whom Hamilton and Burr fought a duel'."*

But Madame could not go out in her carriage freely. Chase kept her in surveillance. The story of her little boy in Providence was hardly a well kept secret, and Chase lived in dread of the time Madame would make a will in favor of George Washington Bowen. But without knowing her son's feelings toward her, Madame felt she could not make an appropriate testament.

Secretly she arranged to have her carriage prepared for the journey to Providence. But Chase was as clever as she, and his resources were superior. Someone in the household set fire to the stables. The old carriage burned; Madame's hope was thwarted forever. She would never make the attempt again, never see her son.

If she despised Nelson Chase, she had little affection for Willy. At fifteen he had eloped with a middle-aged woman who seduced him, hoping to be included in the division of Madame's estate. The ploy was transparent. The Willy Chases lived with Madame and the peace of the house was hard to maintain.

Madame still went to Saratoga for its healing waters and the quiet of the Tuileries. Secure in their power, Chase and his son let her go. Since she could no longer make the journey by carriage, she took the Albany steamer. It was her pleasure. Some felt the voyage was a trip to Paradise. For Madame it was a trip to France. Her cabin was designed as a place of assignation, with mother-of-pearl arches and mirrored walls. She loved the public salons, which were decorated in "the French style" with pink false marble columns and dark walnut paneling. Here she could hold an imaginary court. Even the sight of her was recorded in the journals of several ladies. *"I saw her, a little old lady fantastically dressed and powered and rouged, who smiled and bowed to left and right, for she was the center of all attention. She was in the dining salon, surrounded by dozens of small baskets fluttering with ribbons, while waiters at a little distance nudged each other and exchanged smiles to show it was common knowledge that she was demented."*

The people of Saratoga still found it amusing to harass Madame Jumel. With obscene cruelty, they conspired to teach her a final lesson. The three o'clock parade had become a contest. Fortunes were spent on horses and their equipage, carriages and outriders. Madame had a carriage in Saratoga; at eighty-four, it

188

was still her pride to lead the procession.

Tom Camel, free slave of Bahyte, the hermit, was hired to mock her. He was a white man's black man, always willing to play the fool, famous for sawing himself off the limb of a tree. They dressed him in a low cut gown, with an ostrich plume hat, sat him on a laundry basket in a farm cart, pulled by sway-backed plow horses, ridden by three outriders dressed as green scarecrows - in memory of Madame's green French livery. Madame led the parade; lying back seductively, fanning herself, taking the applause and whistles as her due.

Bowen told the story dryly in Court. *"That was the last time she was in Saratoga,"* he said. *"And they made such a row and the folks stood around saying she was Madame Jumel. And they made such fun of her. I can't tell you how much. There was a hundred people standing around seeing the exhibition. It was in front of the United States Hotel."* He did not tell the court what his mother's humiliation meant to him. She led the parade the following day, crossing her hands in her lap, holding a pistol in either hand. It was her last appearance as Madame Jumel.

Chase was summoned. He did not speak of Madame's ordeal, but referred to *"a natural shock which came to her in Saratoga."* He said she complained of pain and *"things floating before her vision."* Detached cells from the retina float in front of the eyes of many old people. But Madame had intimations of death. In spite of Nelson Chase, she summoned another lawyer, William Wetmore, who summered in Saratoga. She asked Wetmore to draw up a will excluding the Chases and Perys, leaving everything she owned to charity.

"I could not really get out of her what she wanted

189

to do," Wetmore would tell the Court. *"In the beginning, she talked about beqeathing her estate to charity. But she was continuously talking about her life in France, about touring the boulevards, and her acquaintance with the Duchess of Berry and others. I could not pin her mind down."* When he testified, Wetmore had long been an agent of Nelson Chase.

"I brought her home myself," said Nelson Chase. *"And her mind was demented, and as I was taking her back, she sprang from my side and ran up to party of strangers and putting her mouth to their ears, she gave a fearful shriek. And when she got home, she labored under the same mental excitement."*

Madame would explain her withdrawal differently. *"The Tuileries was a delightful retreat,"* she told a young woman who called at the Mansion. *"But Mr. Chase told me the men in the great hotels were making crowns of precious stones for me to wear, to crown me Queen. And I was so frightened that I packed up and returned immediately to New York."* Even in her anguish, she dreamed of refusing a crown.

It was time to summon "les cher enfants," Eliza and Paul Pery to join Chase and Willy in their death watch, to keep Madame in her madness from making another will. Chase ordered them home.

"To M. Jean E. Pery, Notaire, Bordeaux.
My very dear friend:
This letter and the enclosed check are for the dear children, Eliza and Paul. The letter will inform you that Madame Jumel is resolved that they should return to live in this country. And the money is to be applied to their return voyage from Bordeaux to New York.
My letter addressed to Paul and Eliza is explicit.

The money which I am sending is not to be used for any other purpose, but exclusively as the means of assuring their return voyage to this country; and I beg you to impress on them well that the instructions I am giving must be executed to the letter and in full.

I shall have the greatest pleasure in embracing those dear children in this country, and I will spare nothing to ensure their welfare and future success.

Permit me to say in conclusion, my dear friend, to assure you that they will not lack the protection of a father. You will ever command the gratitude and high esteem of your friend and most obliging servant,
Nelson Chase

Madame, the Perys and the Chases lived together briefly and wretchedly. *"I noticed a great change in Madame's mental capacity after my return from France,"* said Eliza Pery. *"She accused me of trying to poison her, saying I kept arsenic in my pocket to put in her tea. After she made these charges, she told me how much she loved me and treated me with affection. But these charges and changes continued until the time of her death."* And, until she died, whenever he was in residence, Nelson Chase was obliged to taste Madame's food before she would eat. She was never fully assured, and to counteract any poison her families could administer, she drank great glasses of sweet oil which she called a 'sovereign remedy,' an antidote to poison and a vaccine against disease.

The Perys, having known freedom, refused to live in the madhouse, and in spite of the rage of Nelson Chase, moved out.

Chase stayed in the Mansion working for his inheritance. Like the Biblical Ruth he was true to his mother-in-law. He went where she went, stayed where she stayed. Her people became his people. He had no other loyalty.

He would attack his daughter in Court for deserting him. He would say of Eliza's withdrawal from the Mansion, that *"her unfair, immoral, and undutiful and vicious conduct had been a cause of grief and oppression and torment to Madame Jumel."*

28

"When the world has once begun to use us ill, it
afterwards continues the same treatment with less
scruple or ceremony, as men do a whore."
Jonathan Swift

Madame could assess the feelings of the Perys
and the Chases. She had only to think of her own
impatience, when Stephen stood between herself and
the illusion of happiness. When she found the screws
which held her heavy wardrobe to the wall, had been
pulled loose and the upper structure pushed forward,
and badly balanced, she accused Willy of setting a death
trap. Her rage was tempered with fear.

"I was her favorite until that time," Willy said.
*"Then one night she came down in a furious passion to
where I was sitting at the supper table and said I had
attempted to assassinate her by unscrewing the wardrobe
so that it would fall on her and kill her. I tried to reason
with her to no purpose and I was compelled to leave the
house."*

In the course of his *"reasoning"*, Willy threw an
ink stand at the Ercole portrait. He aimed for his great
aunt's smiling face but hit his own and broke the
canvas. "Thereafter," said Nelson Chase, *"Madame
Jumel exhibited a monomaniacal diminution of her
regard for and antipathy toward William Chase."* In
court neither Nelson Chase nor Willy spoke of the ink
stand and the broken portrait. But it had mattered to
Madame. As if he no longer existed, she sewed a patch
of black silk over the place where Willey's face had

been. Nevertheless, she set him up in business so that he could support the middle-aged fortune hunter who had married him.

Madame regarded Nelson Chase with similar horror. She gathered energy to treat the Chases, father and son, as she had her second husband. Like Burr, Willy and Nelson came home to find everything they owned thrown out of doors. Like Burr they gathered their things and found other lodgings.

Then Madame lived alone, except for a woman to care for the house and man to keep the grounds. Patrick Carrol, the Mansion's guardian, kept the keys to the gates on his person and slept with a gun under his pillow.

The house grew shabby for want of repair. The paint peeled and windows rattled. Water found its way through the roof. Grounds and gardens returned to their wild state and saplings displaced the pickets of the fence. Then the shutters were permanently closed, so that the passing of one day into another would not remind Madame of coming darkness; and only a crack of light or wisp of smoke betrayed the half-life within to the curious without.

She abandoned all habits of cleanliness and order. The air in the shuttered rooms became offensive. In an effort to control her circumstances, Madame advertised for a companion. An English woman applied for the position, but finding her would-be employer sitting on a throne in a dark room, waiting for a visit from Governor Hoffman, she hurriedly withdrew.

Chase and his children could not afford to leave Madame without surveillance. Eliza Pery visited her regularly. She was often warmly received, although always at some point Madame remembered that Eliza kept arsenic in her pocket and meant to put it in her tea. Willy would testify that, in spite of his eviction, he too visited his great aunt. *"She always welcomed me until she remembered that I had tried to assassinate her,"* he said.

Nelson Chase was never allowed in the house, but he was not helpless. He had long since subverted William Wetmore who agreed to pretend to draw up as many wills as Madame wanted to make. *"After 1857,"* Wetmore said, *"I always wrote whatever she asked me to write, knowing it could never be confirmed as a testament made in her right mind. My object, as a friend of the family,"* he said without shame, *"was to keep control of the old lady, lest if I refuse to do what she said, she might go to another lawyer."*

Madame's will to prevail in her last will and testament was adament. She recognized Wetmore as an agent of Chase and plotted against him. Through Ann Eliza she sent a message to George Washington Bowen saying she was dying, begging him to come, to receive her blessing. *"He replied in an indignant and uncomplimentary manner,"* wrote William Henry Shelton, the Mansion's first curator. Then Madame gave up any hope that her son might love her and having no love to lose, found herself emotionally ready to dispossess everyone she knew.

She summoned Father Smith, the priest at the Chapel of the Intercession, where although she was no longer a communicant she still paid for a pew. Having dsciplined herself to withhold those things which suggest madness, Madame pleaded cleverly. She said she did not expect to live long, that she needed immediate help to draw up a will. She wanted to leave

money for the erection of an Episcopal church in
Harlem Heights. With the innocence of an old
courtesan, she asked if one hundred thousand dollars
would be enough. She asked Smith to draw up a list of
worthy charities, adding that she wanted to add his
name to her list of beneficiaries.

*"I told her I could draw up a list of charities, but
that I must decline any personal legacy,"* said Father
Smith. *"And I told her I wasn't competent to draw up a
will. And she asked me to come again and bring a lawyer
with me who would help her. Again I declined, saying I
did not wish to be involved in a family matter."*

But when the Reverend Howard Smith talked
the matter over with the officers of Trinity Church
(the Chapel of the Intercession is a branch of Trinity in
the Village), they overcame his objections; even his
reluctance to be named as a beneficiary in Madame's
will.

To avoid the charge of conflict of interest, the
officers of Trinity must have discussed the matter with
Nelson Chase, because the lawyer the priest brought
when he called on Madame again, was William
Wetmore. *"Mr. Wetmore went upstairs to where
Madame lay in bed and stayed with her an hour or more
while I waited in the parlor,"* said Father Smith. *"At no
time did I discuss the contents of Madame's will with Mr.
Wetmore."*

When Mr. Wetmore had gone, Madame called
Smith back to her room. *"Father,"* she said, hiding the
fact that she was almost blind, *"that old man writes such
a bad hand I can't read his writing. Will you read the will
to me so I can sign it in your presence?"*

"I did so," Smith said. *"And when I came to the*

bequest for Nelson Chase, she said she meant to leave him ten thousand dollars, not the twenty Mr. Wetmore had written; and she asked me to put it down so. She made a similar remark about the twenty thousand bequest for Mrs. Pery, saying it should be cut in half. And when I came to the bequest for myself, she said that figure was wrong too. She wanted to give me five thousand dollars. And I changed the figure at her direction. But I strongly protested her direction concerning Mrs. Pery. I begged her to let Mr. Wetmore's figure remain.

"She would only waste it," said Madame Jumel. *"Mrs. Pery is a vain and frivolous woman."*

The priest and the mad woman compromised, agreeing to give the Pery woman fifteen thousand dollars. From the list of charities Smith proposed, Madame chose those that evoked memories of sailors and homeless women - memories older than any of the kin who waited for her death. Her largest legatee was the Church of the Intercession, which she rewarded as she had promised, with a gift of one hundred thousand dollars.

Father Smith would testify for Madame Jumel, saying she had been wholly competent and of sound mind when she dictated this, her last will.

That year when she lived alone, physically helpless and plotting to keep the remnants of her power; Madame's neighbor, Mr. Haven, called on her with three young ladies. The visit seems to have been arranged in the spirit that a parent arranges to take children to a national monument. Madame received her visitors with pleasure; and Miss Parker, who had been a guest, went from the Mansion directly to her desk at home.

"I wish to write down the facts connected with my

visit to Madame Jumel in Fort Washington," Miss Parker wrote, *"For the stories she related of herself are so remarkable that I fear in relating them I might either exaggerate or, from fear of drawing too largely on my imagination, fail to do them justice.*

It was with great difficulty that we gained admittance to the place - Mr. Haven, his daughter, Miss Treadwell and myself - although Madame appointed an hour to see us and appeared delighted with the prospect of a visit from young girls.

A second appointment was made after the failure of the first and we found the gate locked as usual. But we sent the footman over the fence, who returned with a message from Madame, saying she was waiting to receive us. And the Irishman came with a heavy key and let us in. I felt as if we had, even within the gates, achieved a great victory.

There she stood on the front steps which were painted with blue moons on a lavender floor. A more fearful old woman one seldom sees. Her hair and teeth were false, her skin thick and possessing no shadow of ever having been handsome and clear. Her feet were enormous; and stockings, soiled and coarse, were wrinkled over her shoes. On one foot she wore a gaiter and on the other a carpet slipper. Her dress, or the skirt, which was all that was visible, was a dyed black silk with stamped flounces, three of them, such as were worn six or eight years ago. It was very rusty and narrow in the skirt. She wore a large hoop, which sitting she could not manage, and it stood up displaying her terrible feet. Over her shoulders she wore a rusty merino scarf around her neck. Her cap was made of humbug, white and blond with black cotton lace and it had long pea green streamers... Such was the sight that greeted us. This was the fabulously wealthy and elegant Madame Jumel, who received such unbounded attention in Europe, not only from nobility but from royalty itself.

She received us as if we were all duchesses and she a queen. She called our attention to the splendid view before we went in. There at our left was the East River and a distant view of High Bridge and New York far below. Her place must have been superb before, and at the time of her marriage to Colonel Burr, but it is sadly neglected now. The house is beautifully planned; two large square halls and a parlor and in back of that, a staircase which is not visible when you enter. Everything looked as if it was many years since they had been dusted, and the atmosphere was very disagreeable, as if fresh air was unknown.

These two halls had inlaid tables choicely and beautifully set in gilt frames, hanging baskets and etageres covered with articles of virtue. These walls were hung with rare paintings. One especially, a full length of General Washington, which was my admiration.

A large painting of a lady and two children, a boy and a girl, hung on the left. The size was enormous and the frame of maroon velvet ornamented with gilt vine, Madame said was her own design. It was a likeness of herself taken in Rome and the children were a niece and a nephew of M. Jumel's. Over the boy's face was sewn a piece of black stuff.

'Aha', said Mr. Haven with his fine old school manners, 'Aha, Madame, what has happened to mar so fine a painting?'

'Sir, she replied, 'I placed that patch there with my own hands. His character is defaced, not the picture, and there it shall remain until he redeems himself.'

The niece, Eliza, met and married when in Europe ten years ago with Madame, a preacher, a Mr. Peri or

Perrer and they live in New York City. She will probably inherit all this fabulous wealth which Madame hoards so carefully.

She led us to the sitting room to the right of the hall where there was a fire on the grate. And I should think from all appearances, she lived in it entirely. The place was chilly, like all places which are never aired and the fire made little difference. Her coachman's livery coat hung on the sideboard, a pair of soiled stockings lay in one corner. On the table was a britannia tray and tea things of the same metal and the relics of a forlorn breakfast - a dirty molasses pot and shabby cake basket, all of britannia.

We were very much afraid that she would invite us to eat something, but she was very magnificent and amiable in her manners and conversation, and called our attention to the paintings on the walls, told us where they were bought, etc.

We were very curious to hear her talk of Aaron Burr, and when she alluded to him incidentally, we asked her if he was at all handsome. 'Ah, my child,' she replied, 'he was a wretch'." Madame told the story of their midnight wedding.

"Who this Chase she speaks of is I do not know. He has a keen black eye. On dit that Chase is a son of Aaron Burr. He is a lawyer and intimate of Charles O'Conor. They two are called the steamboat and the tug." O'Conor was tall and thin; Chase short and stout. "He lived at Fort Washington and looked after her property but interfered too much, Madame said, and when he came home from town one night, he found his luggage and traps all thrown out in a heap on the lawn outside. Since that time, he has lived in town. Madame told us all this.

She said she gave a dinner to wipe out her bad treatment of the King of Spain. Colonel Burr and many

200

distinguished guests were present, and Joseph Bonaparte praised this table so much that she kept it standing to this day.

There in the dining room the table was left - china, glass, still there and the gold ornaments and pyramids of confections still standing on that greasy, dusty table, crumpled and molded. This same table Mrs. Appleton-Haven saw twenty-years ago. It is unchanged now, except that Madame was persuaded by Mrs. O'Conor that it was imprudent to leave so many gold and silver ornaments about, so some of them were put in the safe."

Madame told her callers about her reunion with Napoleon III and how the Duke of Palermo pursued her. " 'My dear,' she said to me, 'I was seventy-two years old'." In truth she was seventy-eight. " 'Think of inspiring such love! Parlez-vous Francais, ma cher?'

'Yes, I said, 'I speak it easily.' And then followed a long conversation in which she joined me with as much ease as if she were twenty or French. She complimented me on my style and pronunciation and told me I should see the Duke's letter, although she did not offer to show it to me.

She asked me if I had ever seen her summer retreat in Saratoga, the Tuileries, and did I think she should go there next summer, and would I go with her.

'Certainly,' I said, and she asked me where she should send me word and I said to Mrs. Haven and that seemed to satisfy her...

From this she went on to talk about the War and her sorrow for our troubles. She betrayed some Southern sympathy which vexed Mr. Haven." He had a son in the Union Army. "Then she told him of a plan she had heard a short time before from Mr. William Astor, who she said, had recognized her team before a shop in town and had gone in to speak to her. He told her that a mighty prophet had appeared...and that before the War came, he foretold how it would come to pass. And, now, he said, the North and South could only be reconciled by making Madame Jumel, queen. What did we think of that?

These stores are among the most remarkable. My patience would be exhausted to write more. We were there for more than two hours, and then could get away only by promising her we would come again very soon. She followed us out to our carriage, telling us her beliefs...and her present faith in the Church and her great belief in the Holy Spirit... She related some marvelous stories of her early life on this place which belonged to her, and her plans for a new house with seven halls lined with mirrors.

She had much to say of the treasure Captain Kidd buried on her place, of the times of the Indian massacre and of General Washington's intimacy at her father's house.

She has but two very inferior servants who have charge of the house, horses and place. Horses are her only luxury. Her meannesses are easily accounted for, as she thinks all who have any interest in her are merely so for her wealth and a desire to make something of her. Her horror of Mr. O'Conor and Mr. Chase seems to be on this account. They strongly advised her to make a will.

It is unfortunate that she has no children to interest and take care of her. A childless and forlorn old age hers has proved to be, in spite of the brilliancy of her youth and more good fortune in her early years than generally falls to us. This verifies my belief that to a certain extent, all things are equal.

In a sense, although not Miss Parker's all things were equal; the wretchedness of Madame's youth was equal to the misery of her old age. She suffered physically as well as mentally, but she could not accept the humanness of frailty. As her functions failed, she elevated her self-image, as if she could balance physical suffering with even greater delusions of grandeur. She assumed the gift of healing and believed she could heal any illness by the application of her hands. But she could not adequately lay hands on herself. When pain racked her, she could only imagine she had been poisoned and does herself with sweet oil.

Toward the end she sometimes was forced to call for help. The first time she called Dr. John Crane, she told him she had eaten twelve quarts of strawberries, and sweet oil would not relieve her distress. Dr. Crane told her she suffered from a surfeit of berries. *"But,"* she_argued, *"it is my habit, Sir, to eat twenty-four boxes of_ berries at a time"* She explained that she had been poisoned.

As she argued, her mind wandered. Talking at random, she said she had been granted a vision of Heaven and described its beauties. As earthly problems drew her back, she said her neighbors on the Heights had tried to rob her. Dr. Crane would testify that such charges against *"families held in the highest esteem,"* were evidence of madness. *"Nevertheless,"* he told the court, *"Madame argued soundly from her premises, such as they were."* He said she suffered from gastric derangement.

Time became Madame's custodian. Her attention turned inward away from wills, the conspiracies of the Chases and the pilfering of her neighbors. As she sat in her dark throne room, only the most immediate necessities moved her. She did not, could not, assimilate her life or deal in retrospect with the moral differences between her self-image and her real nature. But slipping in and out of sleep, rousing from nightmares to hallucinations, perhaps sometimes kings and emperors knelt at her feet and asked for her hand in marriage.

From time to time Nelson Chase came to assure himself that she was alive. But, of course, Madame's servants and Dr. Crane kept Chase informed of the addition of failures which presaged her death. In the summer of 1865, Chase and the young Miss Hattie Denning, with whom he had fallen in love, moved into the Mansion. Then Chase summoned Father Smith telling him to do whatever seemed necessary to induce Madame to write an appropriate will. Probably Chase offered or threatened anything he thought necessary to subvert Smith. But backed by the power of Trinity Church, Smith testified that he would not betray Madame.

Madame weighed no more than a child. Chase carried her to the Bonaparte bed. It's curtains, falling from head and foot, hid her view of the room. She never knew who waited and watched beside her, but Miss Denning fitted her dream. At Madame's request Miss Denning made up the crumpled face. Madame asked to wear her diamonds. Miss Denning dressed her: diamonds on her disheveled wig, her skeletal wrists, her pendulous ears, her gnarled fingers, over the bib of her soiled gown. It suited Miss Denning's dream too.

Madame gave up her ghost. She had been born as the guns of the Revolution sounded at Lexington. She died as the stillness settled at Appomattox, in the ninetieth year of her age.

She was dead (it cannot really be ascertained) when Miss Denning ordered Patrick Carrol to remove her diamonds and bury them in the garden with her other jewels, her silver tea set, her gold and silver plates and her portable Bonaparte treasures. These disposed of, Chase sent Patrick to bring Dr. Crane. Crane brought a young woman with him to look at the corpse. Miss Denning had dressed her suitably. The young woman remembered Madame wore a cap trimmed with pink streamers.

Madame's remains were displayed in a rosewood coffin on the dais which had held her throne. Her kin gathered. Chases and Perys followed her hearse to the Chapel of the Intercession and listened as Father Smith read the Order for the Burial of the Dead. It is not likely that he red the suggested Psalm. "And veryily, every man living is altogether vanity. He heapeth up riches and cannot tell who will gather them."

Chases and Perys walked to the Mausoleum where her coffin was interned. The vault could hold everyone who followed her coffin, and their children as well. But no one chose to lie in death with Madame Jumel.

Those men and women who had depended on her charity, looked forward to the endless resources of her estate. Chase planned to marry Miss Denning. Eliza Pery had fallen in love with a man who wanted to marry her and Willy's wife planned to endure him, briefly for the sake of his inheritance. They all celebrated Madame's death as their birth in freedom.

29

"Law is anything boldly asserted and plausibly
maintained."
Aaron Burr

Assessors were hired to make an inventory of
Madame's personal property. Furniture, carriages, and
horses were valued at $12,387. She had $3,645 in the
bank and a promissory notice for $18,240. Her stocks
and bonds, jewels, flatware, gold and silver dishes,
statuary, Empire furniture, Bonaparte bed, and
Bonaparte chairs disappeared between the time of her
death and the arrival of the assessors. Some of her kin
were satisfied. All of them knew her real fortune lay in
real estate.

Lawyers opposing the Chases and Perys, that is
lawyers working for George Washington Bowen and
Ann Eliza, would allege in striking detail, that the
treasures buried in Madame's garden that night were
removed by van, with the Bonaparte furniture, to the
home of Julius Caryl in Yonkers. Caryl who would
eventually marry Eliza Pery, was already a wealthy
man. Madame's treasures were either buried again on
his estate or hidden in the sanctity of a safe deposit box.

The expectant kin met and read Madame's will.
Father Smith and the Chapel of the Intercession were
rewarded.   Nelson Chase and the Perys were
remembered with token bequests.   There was no
reference to Willy and his wife. Most of Madame's
fortune was left to those charities which reminded her
of her childhood, her mother and unknown father: The
New York Asylum for Orphans, The Society for the

Relief of Respectable, Aged, Indigent Females, The Missionary Society for Seamen...

Chase immediately seized Madame's papers and claimed her estate, saying he inherited it from his wife Mary, for whom everything was held in trust. Then Willy and his wife, and the Perys, believing there was strength in union, moved into the Mansion with Nelson Chase - as if joint occupancy would demonstrate their joint right to everything that had belonged to Madame Jumel.

Fourteen days after Madame's death, the last of the letters she exchanged with the Bureau of Veteran's Affairs was opened by Nelson Chase.

> *Madame:*
> *Copious difficulties make it impossible to proceed. The matter of Colonel Burr's pension remains to be seen... "*

Burr's pension could not be recovered, but Chase and his children believed the will could be broken. They jointly hired two prominent lawyers, Charles O'Conor and James Carter, and assigned them the task of proving Madame insane and her last testament void. To ease these proceedings, Chase paid Father Smith five thousand dollars and Trinity Church seventy thousand. Smith and Trinity withdrew from the contest.

Meanwhile lawyers, fascinated by the complications of the case made exploratory expeditions to Williamston, Rutland, Saratoga and Providence hoping to complicate the case further with new and competitive heirs. In the first year of litigation - it took a year to break Madame's will - an extraordinary number of claimants brought opposing suits.

The children and grandchildren of Lavinia Ballou Jones sued. Curiously, to a contemporary mind, which does not find illegitimacy horrifying, Lavinia's kin said they were descendants of Polly Clarke rather than Phebe Bowen - Polly Clarke, who either was or could not be proved not to be, the legitimate daughter of Jonathan Clarke and his unknown Boston wife. Madame had not known her grand nieces; nor, if they were descendants of Polly Clarke, were they related to her by blood. But, such was the stringency of the law against bastards, that they all chose to fight with this pedigree; as the descendants of Polly Clarke. These grand nieces of Madame, all with the surname Jumel-Jones, and all named Eliza, had a strong claim. They were born in wedlock. No one claiming blood relationship could suggest as much.

But the identity of the Jumel-Bowen-Ballou-Clarke women shifted as they tried either to clarify or, if it seemed to their benefit, to confuse their relationships. Betsy Bowen's sister Polly was, they said, called Mary or Maria; her last name was Bowen or Bowne, or Brown or Bones. Lavinia Ballou was known as Polly; and Polly Clarke was called Maria Bowne. Betsy, who would become Madame Jumel, was, they said, known as Polly. It would not be appropriate to lead a reader further astray. The identity of the fathers of Lavinia and Betsy and Polly, either Bowen or Clarke, was often argued, but never clarified. Apparently the names of Caleb Bowen's daughters Polly and Betsy, born in Providence, were brought forward solely for the sake of confusion.

Nevertheless the records are straightforward. Phebe (nee Bowen) Clarke bore three daughters, Polly, Lavinia and Betsy; all of them were illegitimate. Like the others, Madame's adopted Mary was born out of wedlock. Ann Eliza Ballou said Mary was Lavinia's child. *"She was the daughter of my mother by another man to whom I suppose she was married. I often saw Mary with Madame. And my mother always said, 'There goes Betsy with the one she brought up'."* But Lavinia was not married when Mary was born. Mary was not legitimate and this stood between her husband, Nelson Chase, and their daughter, Eliza Pery - and any claim they had to Madame's estate.

So well did Chase understand the threat of the four Jumel-Jones to the legitimacy of his suit, that thirty days after Madame's death, he borrowed forty thousand dollars to buy quit claims from them. At the same time, although he was deeply in debt, as well as arrears in taxes, he borrowed an additional five thousand dollars for personal pleasure. Sure that Madame's estate could support any indulgence, assured that the Jumel-Jones had been finally paid off, he married young Hattie Denning and left for Europe on an extended honeymoon.

His happiness was premature. The New York Court which found Madame's will invalid because she was mad, also held that by virtue of wedlock, the Jumel-Jones were the sole heirs to Madame's estate; and citing Mary's illegitimacy, the Court set aside all the transfers of property Madame had made to Mary using Stephen's power of attorney.

Immediately the Jumel-Jones, who had let themselves be legally represented by Nelson Chase, sued to have their quit claims set aside, claiming in perfect truth, that Chase had never appraised them of their rights. Finally, the Jumels of Bordeaux, learning that Madame's estate had been appraised at ten million dollars, and that nothing Madame had accomplished using Stephen's power of attorney was still valid, brought fourteen claims against all the American suitors.

Chase hurried home. From that time one, for the next sixteen years, the so-called 'resident heirs,' the Nelson and Willy Chases and the Eliza Perys, lived together in an atmosphere of mutual loathing, prisoners of the Mansion, just as Madame had been in her failing power. The wretchedness of the families forced to share the Mansion-cage, was exacerbated by Madame's ghost. The force of her misery and frustration had not been dissipated by her death. She paid them nightly visits.

Evidence of Madame's haunting is found in the vivid account of Mlle. Nitschke, who was hired as a governess for little Matilde Pery. The phenomena she describes were almost universally accepted then as manifestations of the dead. Scientists, statesman and intellectuals, as well as the naïve and credulous, passionately believed in the twilight world of ghosts. In this atmosphere, spirits responded as if they had longed for attention from the living. In countless darkened rooms, here and in Europe, spirits made themselves known with rapping noises and cold clouds of ectoplasm; or when more complicated messages were invited, through the vocal cords of mediums.

"I came to live in the Mansion three years after Madame Jumel died," Mlle. Nitschke told William Henry Sheldon. *"My room was on the third floor and the school room was on the third floor. But at any moment, Mrs. Pery might snap the whip under the window and call us to drive in a rattle-trap wagon.*

At this time Nelson Chase would rise at five

o'clock and make the halls ring with his profanity, calling for his breakfast. Nelson Chase at one time, the Pery's at another, and Will Chase and his family still later. The three families were not on speaking terms. I was told not to speak to Mrs. Will Chase or her children. After a little time I was moved down to the Lafayette room to be nearer to Mrs. Pery, who was in nightly terror of the ghost of Madame Jumel which she claimed came with terrible rappings between twelve and one o'clock or about midnight.

Mrs. Pery would come to my room in the night in great excitement to escape the ghost. I would ask her if she did not fear to leave her daughter, but she said Matilde slept soundly and never heard it. One night she insisted on my coming in their bedroom and awaiting the ghost. I always told them there was no such thing as a ghost.

On that particular night, the trouble began as early as seven o'clock in the evening. They had just come up from supper when Mrs. Pery rushed into the hall trembling with fright and calling, 'Mademoiselle!' She had heard or seen some manifestation by which she claimed to know the ghost was going to make a night of it.

At about the same time, probably hearing the cries, Mr. Pery came upstairs from the kitchen where he had been toasting cheese. He disliked to sleep in the room in question, claiming that Madame Jumel had come to his side of the bed dressed in white. At my suggestion they sent for the gardener who lived in one of the gate houses as an additional witness. With his help, I expected to prove to them that what they thought they heard, they had not heard at all.

It was a still night outside, a warm September night without a breath of wind and it was also very quiet inside as the hour grew on to midnight. No one had broken the silence for some moments by a spoken word. Mr. Pery was pretending to read a book. He was seated in the middle of

211

the room in a light chair with nothing around the legs to conceal anything.

Suddenly there were loud raps like the sound of a mallet striking the floor, and directly, seemingly, under Mr. Pery's chair, from which he leapt as if he had been shot.

I had told them when the ghost came to ask if it wished to have prayers said for it. So I put the question, 'Do you want to have prayers said for you?' This was answered by three knocks, which is rap language for yes. The raps that answered to yes and no seemed to be in the walls, now on one side of the room and now on the other. The manifestations as I stated began with heavy raps on the floor under Mr. Pery's chair, and they were followed by a clatter of what sounded like a skeleton hand drumming on the panes of the east front window.

At one time during the manifestations this drumming by the skeleton hand seemed to come from the room where Matilde slept, but the clatter seemed to be on tin instead of glass. I stepped to the door to look in. Even as I looked, the tapping continued on the tin slop pail and then ceased altogether. The child was sleeping soundly, and Mrs. Pery thought I was very brave to enter the room at all."

Mlle. Nitscheke stayed with the Perys another nine months.

The lives of the resident heirs grew more bitter. To avoid the ghost of his mother-in-law, Paul Pery drank himself senseless. Nelson Chase, grown fat and foul-mouthed, tried with Hattie's help to oust his son and daughter, with their families, from the Mansion. Assuming parental authority, Charles O'Conor restored the Paul Perys and Willy Chases, but ousted young Mrs. Nelson Chase because her presence mocked her husband's claim of devotion to his dead wife, Mary.

Both attorneys for the resident heirs found

Nelson Chase so loathsome, that Charles O'Conor, because or in spite of the fact that he was the more famous and forceful of the two, agreed to forfeit a quarter of his fee if Carter would handle the necessary confrontations with Chase. Chase could pay neither lawyer a retainer, but they were content knowing their fees would take precedence in the division of Madame's estate.

Over a period of sixteen years, twenty cases at law were won by the resident heirs, including Willy's suit to expel his father from the house. Thirty-eight suits to eject them all, were brought by the legitimate and illegitimate descendants of Phebe Bowen and Jonathan Clarke (in spite of the fact that they had no children in common). But the definitive and most dramatic conflict in this multiplicity of conflicts was the contest between Nelson Chase and George Washington Bowen. Bowen's existence as Madame's son was common knowledge. As his advocate declaimed before the Court, *"Everyone knows a bastard issued from her womb."*

Before he married and sailed on his honeymoon, Nelson Chase called on Lavinia's daughter Ann Eliza to ask about Madame's bastard. *"Look no further,"* she said, *"George Washington Bowen is Madame's son."*

Chase said he knew it. *"But,"* he said, *"Bowen's illegitimacy makes his claim less than the furthest stranger in the world."* Nevertheless Chase was uneasy and asked Ann Eliza if she had any papers which could be used as proof of Bowen's identity. *"No,"* she said, withholding from Chase both the Henry book where Reuben Ballou recorded Bowen's birth (she had pasted it up as a scrap book), and her own Bible, where she had written the whole complicated family history.

She offered the books to George Washington Bowen instead. He said, " *No thank you. I know enough about by mother without looking in books.*" Then, since Ann Eliza's claim to Madame's estate seemed as good as his own, in a naïve burst of generosity, he gave her a paper saying:
"All Money recovered in the Case of Madame Jumel, recovered by me, will be divided equal between myself and Ann Eliza Vandervort.

Signed, George Washington Bowen."

His lawyer Chauncey Shaffer would tell him this was not a legal document.

Meanwhile the men and women who had known Madame Jumel as Betsy Bowen, the mother of George, were octogenarians. Lawyers from both sides scurried to get depositions before they died.

They found Daniel Hull by accident. *"I was sitting in close to the stove in the evening when they rapped at my door,"* he said. *"One of my neighbors was showing the man where I lived and I went to the door and asked him 'What?' And he says, 'I'm picking up the oldest man in Providence.'*

'Well,' says I, 'I'm old enough and ugly enough.' And he burst out laughing and I asked him in. 'Pears to me there was two or three of 'em.

Says he, 'We're picking up the heirs of Madame Jumel's property'.

'Well,' says I, 'I can tell you who he is right off.' Says I, 'George Washington Bowen,' And I asked him Madame's name - 'Wasn't her name Betsy Bowen?'

'Yes,' says he.

'And didn't she marry a Frenchman in New York?'

214

'Yes,' says he.

'Then they telegraphed right back to New York, that's what they told me, that they had found the heir. And one of them lawyers was Mr. Morton. And I says to him, 'I suppose you don't know me, but you and me used to belong to the Old Guard a long time ago, in the War of 1812.'

Well, they come to my house the next morning. Says I, 'Why did you come here last night?'

For,' says I, 'I couldn't sleep a wink last night thinking it over.' Says I, 'What did Bowen say to you?'

Says he, 'He told me you know who his mother was better than he did. And,' says he, 'if we get the case, I'll give you something pretty handsome.' That warmed me tight up. It did me fifty dollars worth of good when it came out, and that's the whole of it."

"Why, I wouldn't be bribed for all the world," he told the court when Chase's lawyer baited him about the sum.

In 1867 Bowen was told by Judge Edmunds that according to New York law, an illegitimate child could inherit his mother's estate if there were no living legitimate children. The law had been on the books for sixteen years, but no lawyer had told Bowen of his rights. He himself found the circumstances of his birth so painful that he could hardly acknowledge his position. He would not say the word bastard.

"Why you must make that out as you have a mind to," said Bowen as if bastard were an epithet instead of a description of his legal status. "If I have no father and mother, I don't want no slurs put on me."

"Are you a bastard?"

"I wasn't born legitimate, if that's what you mean."

215

"Are you a bastard?"

"Yes," said Bowen.

"It may be difficult for a bastard of eighty-four or five to provide from whose womb he issued, but it's not impossible," said Chauncey Shaffer, arguing for Bowen. *"It's not as long a time as lapsed between the making of Adam and the birth of Moses. It can be done."*

When Bowen was assured by Judge Edmund that his claim to his mother's estate was valid, and took precedence over the claims of the resident heirs, he hired a carriage and drove to the Heights to look at the Mansion he believed was his birthright. It is not likely that the dour old man felt more than resentment; or that he knew he was more fortunate than those surrogate children his mother had raised in luxury. He approached the gate house and told Mrs. Wilkie, who lived there with her husband, that he wished to see the house of his mother, Madame Jumel. Mrs. Wilkie ran to the Mansion.

"Tell your husband to lock the gates and keep the Bowen bastard out," said Eliza Chase Pery Bowen retreated. He never entered the house that Madame had longed to give him.

Chase was dismayed at Bowen's audacity. His attorneys soothed him, saying they did not doubt their ability to repel the bastard's attempt. Nevertheless they told him to ingratiate himself with, or to intimidate, Madame's former servants; to make sure that no one of them would dare repeat in court those often repeated stories about the little boy in Providence.

Elizabeth Freeman and her son Aaron still lived in the Tuileries in Saratoga, caring for the estate in lieu of rent just as they had in Madame's lifetime. Chase

216

came to subvert their testimony and ensure their silence.

Chauncey Shaffer took Mrs. Freeman's deposition after Chase's visit: *"I knew Madame Jumel and she put me in charge of her cottage in Saratoga, taking care of it ,"* she said, *"and they never had no losses after I took charge. I had conversations with Madame Jumel about Mr. Bowen. I first saw him in the fall after she died. He walked into the cottage and said he wanted to look. And after he turned to go away, I thought his shoulders kind of looked like Madame's and he sort of wagged off like her.*

Then I met Mr. Chase in Saratoga. He said he wanted me to come to the American Hotel to see him; and he said he guessed I should not have such hard times. At the Hotel steps, he took my old black hand and led me up to the Hotel and asked me to take off my things. He rang the bell and the porter came up. There was something poured out, but I refused to drink. Then he asked me about my place of birth and my age. Then he asked me where I saw George Washington Bowen and I told him it wasn't the first time I had heard of him. Told him how Madame said she had a son and he might come. I got that out and he stopped me.

He said I was a god damned liar and he knocked me down there on the table so that every glass was all bounding, and he said if I was going to talk like that to get out. I said I was going as fast as I could. I left and after I got downstairs, Mr. Chase opened the window and said I'd better look out or he would send me and my son to State Prison. "

Aaron Freeman had gone with his mother to Chase's room. He recognized the drink Chase poured as champagne and guessed the white woman with

217

Chase was his wife.

Elizabeth Freeman continued: *"It was Mr. Chase that put me out on the 20th of January. I didn't know anybody had authority but him. And an officer put me out of the house. He was the high sheriff and he fetched a great long paper then and read so many name I never heard of, but Mr. Chase's name was on it. And it was bitter cold and the snow was dreadful deep."* Such were the racial morés that she felt compelled to add. *"I was not mad at Mr. Chase."*

Among the things thrown out in the snow were half a dozen lithographs of the portrait Madame had made in Paris. *"They was tossing about,"* said Elizabeth, *"and I picked some up and put them in my trunk. And afterward, I gave two or three to Mr. Shaffer."*

Chauncey Shaffer took Elizabeth's deposition shortly after she was evicted. Because she was homeless and sympathetic to his client, as well as able and honest, he took her into his home as a servant. She was asked if Shaffer paid for the lithographs. *"I do think he gave a return for them"* she said, *"because one day when I was out he left a pair of ducks and a pair of turkeys. I do think that is what they was for."* She proved a better witness for Bowen than for Chase.

Nevertheless in 1873, Judge Shipman of the United States Circuit Court for the Southern District of New York dismissed the evidence of Madame's servants as hearsay. The persuasive testimony of Daniel Hull was called hearsay also, and the record of Bowen's birth in the Henry book was disposed of as forgery.

Judge Shipman's prejudice was stronger than O'Conor's who surely recognized Bowen's identity when he shook his fist at him and shouted, "You bastard!" Having disposed of the evidence, Shipman told the jury that the burden of proof lay on George Washington Bowen. *"If he has proved to your satisfaction beyond a shadow of a doubt that he is Madame's son, then he is entitled to the verdict."* The jury deliberated for an hour and a half before they agreed that Bowen was not the son of Madame Jumel and the resident heirs should divide the spoils. It was a milestone in jurisprudence, the longest civil case ever tried in the United States.

But it was far from over. Bowen applied to the Supreme Court of New York saying that his rights as a citizen of Rhode Island had been violated. The resident heirs were New Yorkers and he was not. The Court upheld his plea and he took the case to the Supreme Court of the United States.

Meanwhile the cast changed. Paul Pery died, freeing Eliza Pery to marry Julius Caryl - in whose back yard it was alleged that Madame's treasure was buried. Caryl moved into the Mansion.

The United States Supreme Court met to decide three questions: Was Bowen Madame's son? Were Madame's deeds and conveyances to Mary Junel Chase legal; or was Madame's tenure a life-estate which expired at her death? And if Madame's conveyances were in fact legal, and if in fact Bowen was Madame's son, which contestant had the superior claim?

The Supreme Court confirmed the verdict of the New York Court. Bowen was not Madame's son. The pretender was charged court costs for his impudence.

In 1880 Willy Chase paid quit claims to the Jumels of Bordeaux. All claims were settled in 1881, when the Mansion was sold at public auction.

Madame's acres were divided into seven hundred and thirty three house lots; the income to be divided equally between Nelson Chase, his son Willy and his daughter, Eliza Pery Caryl.

It was too late. After sixteen years there was nothing to divide except debt. Charles O'Conor's fee was $300,000; James Carter, a quarter more, for he had had the odious task of dealing with Nelson Chase. Smaller sums were divided between lesser lawyers. Madame's holdings in Saratoga, France, Malta and New York City, disappeared, like her diamonds, between the arrangements of lawyers and the contrivances of her heirs.

The City demanded satisfaction for mortgages given as security for loans, for arrears in taxes, for interest accrued on those arrears, and for assessments for improvements made on Madame's property. Interest on the forty-five thousand dollars Chase had borrowed to buy quit claims form the Jumel-Jones had grown too. He owed seventy three thousand dollars in interest on that alone.

The lawyers had finished their sport with the heirs. Madame's revenge was complete.

Epilogue

George Washington Bowen lived to be ninety. His thin mouth, strong nose, small eyes and projecting brow carried the family myth forward, and the story of George Washington begetting a child on Betsy Bowen became as real as if it were true. He died in Providence four years after his mother's estate was settled. His ill-fated claim passed then to his cousin, John Reuben Vandervoort. For the next eighteen years Vandervoort made a poor living selling quit claims to anyone who bought property on Harlem Heights.

This obituary appeared in the **Providence Evening Tribune** on April 19, 1920:

Miss Ida Bowen, formerly of the City, thirty-seven years old and the great grand daughter of the famous Madame Jumel, and thus able to trace her ancestry directly to George Washington, committed suicide by hanging, Saturday night at the Morris Plains Hospital for the Insane in New Jersey."

Julius Caryl, who married Eliza Pery, was a wealthy man, a member of the New York Stock Exchange and a founder of the Susquehanna Railroad. Nevertheless, he spent the first twelve years of his marriage living with the families of Willy and Nelson Chase in the haunted Mansion. In 1881, when the house irrevocably passed from the family, the Caryls moved first to Yonkers and then to the Tuileries in Saratoga. There was no truer daughter of the Revolution than Phebe Bowen's daughter Betsy. But to avoid the taint of illegitimacy, Eliza Chase Pery Caryl called herself the great grandchild of Jonathan Clarke and the wife he left behind in Boston. As such she was made the Honorary President of the Saratoga Chapter of the Daughters of the American Revolution.

Every summer she draped the Tuilleries with flags and bunting. Finally on Valentine Day, 1903, she re-enacted, as best she could, the presentation of the eagle to the Army on the Champs de Mars; the pageant which had so impressed her as an adolescent, watching the curtain rise on the Second Empire. She had a banner made displaying the emblem of the Daughters on blue silk with gold fringes. The D.A.R. did not respond as ceremoniously as the Citizen's Corps of Utica had to Madame's banner, but they hung Mrs. Caryl's flag in their monument, Constitution Hall in the nation's capitol.

The treasures Mr. Caryl buried or hid on the night that Madame died, were introduced without a hint of scandal almost forty years later in Saratoga. The jewel box painted by the Empress Josephine, her gold and enamel watch, the back comb she wore at her coronation, the mahogany table where Louis Philippe played chess with Madame Jumel, the little box Marie Antoinette carried to the Bastile, the Emperor's sideboard, his clock with the gold sculpted gods, his battle chest, his narrow bed... everything was admired in perfect innocence.

"Guests lingered long to examine the Napoleonic treasure, pieces of Napoleon and the Empress Josephine," wrote the society editor of the Saratoga paper on the occasion of the Caryl's silver wedding anniversary. *"Wearing her wedding gown, mrs. Caryl appeared at the head of the stairs. She descended to the strains of 'Hear*

Comes the Bride' to receive a nuptual blessing and a silver cup, the gift of the Daughters of the American Revolution." Thus on the arm of her husband, Eliza Caryl entered society and buried the story of her great aunt.

In 1894, the Jumel Mansion was refurbished. Its fine Colonial mantels were torn out, its ceilings papered over. The woodwork in the parlor was painted red; and by breaking through the attic for north light, General Washington's office was made into an artist's studio. Radical changes were made in the slave quarters and basement kitchen.

In 1903, Eliza Caryl, giddy with pleasure at the presentation of her banner, urged the Washington Heights Chapter of the Daughters to buy the Jumel Mansion. They did, perhaps because it had been Washington's Headquarters rather than Madame's pride. They restored the house to its Federal beauty. Certainly it is fitting that the Daughters are custodians of the Mansion. It has always been a woman's house. It was built for Washington's sweetheart, Mary Philips. Madame won it as a femme sole and she possesses it in spirit still.

Some believe the house is haunted. The Mansion's third curator, Mrs. Le Roy Campbell, told ghost stories freely. She explained to anyone who asked that the room on the third floor is locked because anyone with a weak heart could die of terror there. "The D.A.R. can't be responsible." At Campbell's instigation, the psychic Sybl Leek came to the house and called it haunted.

In 1964, on the anniversary of Stephen's death, the ghost hunter, Hans Holzer, held a seance in Madame's room in the presence of many reporters.

Madame, using a medium's vocal cords topped the seance. *"Go from my house,"* she shouted. *"I am the lady of the house. I am the wife of the Vice President of the United States. Prying fool. Go or I'll have you put out. You're not wanted, you bastard."*

Campbell's credulity was sometimes abused. I've judged her stories in that context. Nevertheless, I too believe the house is haunted. One rainy morning I heard something beat on the door of the locked room on the third floor; and I left the Mansion too frightened to think I would ever return, which is the reason I did.

Ghostly rapping is usually explained as the unconscious projection of a hysterical personality. Obviously Campbell identified herself with Madame's myth. Any reference to Madame's thwarted social ambitions annoyed her. *"Why would a cultivated woman, familiar with the courts of France, want the company of New York hicks?"* she would ask rhetorically.

But the phenomena did not end with Campbell's stewardship. Working at a table in the great hall on the second floor, I watched the lights in Madame's room wax and wane all day. Toward evening I stood by Madame's door and was engulfed in fragrance. I thought of fresh flowers rather than perfume. I spoke to Jane Crowley, the curator, who was still working at her desk. Together we went to Madame's room. Strands of fragrance hung in the air like spider webs. I followed a thread to Madame's dressing table, opened a drawer, took out a rusty black fan. At that moment the lights faded, leaving us wholly in the dark. It was a winter afternoon; the sun had set. We waited without speaking until, as slowly as they had ebbed, the lights returned.

I smelled that same fragrance twice again. Once by Madame's door and once on the third floor in a storage room where I sat on the floor reading a box of letters written by Aaron Burr.

Perhaps Madame's ghost has been appeased. On the bicentennial of American Independence, the British monarch, Elizabeth II and her husband Philip visited the Mansion. As they explored its rooms; admiring or professing to admire its graceful proportions and the sanctity of its relics, Madame's hopes must have been realized. At least I hope they were.

Bibliography

THE JUMEL MANSION. William Henry Shelton. Houghton Mifflin. 1916.

HISTORY OF RUTLAND. New England Magazine. Vol.8. August, 1893.

STREETS OF THE CITY: An Anecdotal History of Providence. F. L. Simester. Mansion House. 1968.

THE OLD STONE BANK HISTORY OF PROVIDENCE, RHODE ISLAND. John W. Haley. Vol.4 Providence Institute for Savings. 1944.

MOREAU de St. MERY'S AMERICAN JOURNEY. Translated by Kenneth Roberts and Anna M. Roberts. Doubleday & Co. 1947.

THE DISCOVERY OF THE ASYLUM: SOCIAL ORDER AND DISORDER. David J. Rathman. Little Brown & Co. 1971.

WPA HISTORY OF SOUTH CAROLINA: WILLIAMSTON.

GEORGE WASHINGTON. James Thomas Fleschner. New American Library. 1973.

PORTRAITS OF ST. MEMIN. APPLETON MAGAZINE. Charles Kasson Wead, 1906.

TRAVELS THROUGH AMERICA IN 1780, 1781, 1782. Francois Jean, Marquis de Chastellux, London. 1787.

TRAVELS OF FOUR AND A HALF YEARS IN THE UNITED STATES OF AMERICA: 1798, 1799, 1800, 1801, & 1802. John Davis, New York. 1909

THE STREETS OF OLD NEW YORK. Earnest Brierly. Hastings House. 1953.

THIS WAS NEW YORK: THE NATIONS CAPITOL, 1789. Frank Monahan. Doubleday & Doran. 1943.

THE WEALTH & BIOGRAPHY OF THE WEALTHY CITIZENS OF THE CITY OF NEW YORK. Moses Yale Beach. 1844.

THE REPUBLICAN COURT, OR AMERICAN SOCIETY IN THE DAYS OF WASHINGTON. N.Y. 1867.

THE CITY OF NEW YORK IN THE YEAR OF WASHINGTON'S INAUGURATION. Thomas E. Smith. 1889.

THE FIRST FORTY YEARS OF AMERICAN SOCIETY: PORTRAYED IN THE FAMILY LETTERS OF MRS. MARGARET BAYARD SMITH. N.Y. 1906.

OLD NEW YORK. Henry Collins Brown. E.P. Dutton & Co. 1934.

HISTORY OF CHURCHES IN NEW YORK CITY.
Greenleaf. 1807.

OLD ST. PATRICKS. Mother Mary Peter Carthy.
United States Catholic Historical Society. Vol. 23.

THE STORY OF A STREET: A NARRATIVE
HISTORY OF WALL STREET FROM 1644-1908.
Frederick Trevor Hill.
JUMEL & DESORBY: Account Book.

THE SECRET HISTORY OF THE HORRORS OF
SANTO DOMINGO IN A SERIES OF LETTERS
WRITTEN BY A LADY AT CAPE FRANCAIS TO
COL. AARON BURR. Philadelphia. 1808.

TRANSCRIPT OF RECORD, Number 312. Supreme
Court of the United States.

COURT OF COMMON PLEAS. April, 1868. Chase
vs. Bowen.

CITIZEN TOUSSAINT. Ralph Korngold. Little
Brown & Co. 1944.

THE FRENCH REVOLUTION. Walter Geer.
Plimpton Press. Norwood, MA.

THE LIFE AND TIMES OF AARON BURR. James
Parton. Mason Bros. 1859.

MEMOIRS OF AARON BURR: Edited by Mathew
L. Davis. Harper & Bros. 1837.

AN ANSWER TO ALEXANDER HAMILTON'S
LETTER CONCERNING THE PUBLIC
CONDUCT AND CHARACTER OF JOHN
ADAMS. James Cheetham. New York. 1800.

DESULTORY REFLECTIONS ON THE NEW
POLITICAL ASPECTS OF PUBLIC AFFAIRS.
John Ward Fenno. New York. 1800.

QUEENS OF AMERICAN SOCIETY. Philadelphia.
1867.

WPA HISTORY OF NEW JERSEY; HOBOKEN.

THE TURBULENT CITY; PARIS, 1783-1871. Andre
Castelot. Harper & Row.

SIX SUMMERS IN PARIS, 1789-94. John Fisher.
Harper & Row.

NAPOLEON. Andrew Castelot. Harper & Row.

THE GOLDEN BEES. Theo. Aaronson. New York
Graphic Society. 1964.

THE AGE OF NAPOLEON. J. Christopher Herold.
American Heritage Publishing Co.

THE LAST DAYS OF NAPOLEON'S EMPIRE.
Henry Lachauque. Orion Press. 1967.

COL. WILLIAM DUSENBURY CRAFT; Interview
by John Stillman, M.D., June 12, 1882. Library of
Congress.

DIVORCE PAPERS: Eliza Burr vs. Aaron Burr.
Circuit Court in Chancery, N.Y.C.

MEMOIRS OF MRS. M. M. COGHLAN. Morrell.
1864.

THE SOCIAL LADDER. Mrs. John King Rensselaer.
Henry Holt & Co. 1924.

CHRONICLES OF SARATOGA AND
BALLSTONE. Stone. 1875.

LEE'S GUIDE TO SARATOGA, N.Y. 1885.

A HISTORY OF MALTA DURING THE FRENCH
AND BRITISH OCCUPATION: 1798-1815.
W.Hardman. London. 1909.

THE FRENCH IN MALTA: Quarterly Magazine.
Victor F. Denaro. 1963.

ASSOCIATION OF THE BAR OF THE CITY OF
NEW YORK: Depository 1832-1881.

THE IMPERIAL MASQUERADE: THE PARIS OF
NAPOLEON III. C.S. Burchell. Atheneum. 1971

THE IMPERIAL SUNSET: 1813-14. R. F. Delerfield.
Chilton Book Co.

ABOUT THE AUTHOR

After graduating from the Yale School of Fine Arts, rather than facing life as a mural painter, Marianne Hancock joined the Red Cross where she served in England until VE Day and then in France with unhappy troops waiting to go to the Pacific. Her First book, **The Perimeter**, is based on that experience.

Later when it was apparent that writing was the only artistic discipline compatible with raising children, she turned to journalism, working as an art critic for *Arts Magazine*, as a drama critic for *Country Magazine* and feature writer for various newspapers and magazines in New York and Connecticut.

Some secrets are safe from any biographer. Chance may eliminate a vital witness or burn a letter that could have opened the flood gates of understanding. Madame of the Heights is as true as two years of research and two years of the author's inner search could discover.

She has lived in Maine with her husband for many years.